T0166862

Photo: Kornelia Jeinke © 2004

Giti Thadani is an interdisciplinary scholar
and lecturer based in New Delhi and Berlin.

MOEBIUS TRIP

Giti Thadani

SPINIFEX

Spinifex Press Pty Ltd
504 Queensberry Street
North Melbourne, Vic. 3051
Australia
women@spinifexpress.com.au
http://www.spinifexpress.com.au

First published by Penguin Books India 2003
This edition published by Spinifex Press, 2004

Typeset in *Adobe Garamond* by Claire Warren, Melbourne
Printed by McPherson's Printing Group

CIP
Thadani, Giti 1961– .
    Moebius Trip.
    Rev. ed.
    ISBN 1 876756 54 3.

    1. India – Antiquities. I. Title.
934

For
Grazia Gonik

ACKNOWLEDGEMENTS

Each part of each journey brings with it its own companions and guides, visible and invisible. Many have their presence in the text itself.

To acknowledge another few:

Betteke Pal, with whom the driving journey first began.

Rosangela Gramoni for her gift of my trusty jeep, the Gypsy. For the many shared travelling experiences.

Letizia Comba for the sharing of another kind of interiority, writings and the long discussions on Rumi.

Elfi Mikesch and Lilly Gröte for the generous use of their apartment in the final stages of the manuscript.

Meher Mistry for making me see Mumbai in another light.

Fareed Curmally for another kind of interlinking.

Yatish Satija for other vital practical aspects.

The writing of the manuscript has followed its own independent trajectory, yet there have been some very special readers. Pervin Mahoney and Sean Mahoney for their detailistic attentivity and the idea of the title.

Grazia Gonik and Ravni Thakur, who received the different partitions as and when.

Writing always demands a savage solitude, particularly in its last stages. Another process starts upon its completion to its eventual publication.

Alain Rivière for being a constant reading and writing companion—for sharing a passion for the same metièr.

Writing and editing often end up on different tracks, yet there occurs another kind of collusion of meticulousness, for which I'd like to acknowledge my editor, Christine Cipriani.

It is very rare for a writer to have a second edition of her work that is further enhanced and fine tuned. For this gift, I'd like to acknowledge Susan Hawthorne in the many capacities of a publisher, writer and reader.

PART I

Seven boundaries/thresholds [maryada], the internal fire described as the one fulcrum to whom one may come; supporting the optimal home, the bearer of the crossroads.

—*Rig Ved*

the first waters became visible, the first parting of the waves,
    the vibrations of the tides, the barque appearing on the
    horizon-azure.
the movements of water, the pathways of the barque floating
    across the invisible passages.

the image became more and more vivid, the pain worse.
the movement that cried for continuation as the body
    contorted itself, bent, unable to withstand the surging flow,
    the current of pain, blood and water.

the azure deepened, the waters still.
the barque continuing its journey, leaving its own trace.
vibrant red lines, contrasting the azure blue.

the colours slowly seemed to change, as if dancing to a
    strange melody that wove its way across the thresholds of

pain, of the boundaries, as if it marked the invitation to cross over.

the image became bleak opaque, the colours disappearing into undecipherable lines.

sounds returned, familiar accessible, the shore receded further away, melting away into oblivion.
sights returned, again accessible, known, visible in all their finitude.

the numbness of the pain remained, as if still pulling at the inner mental frames.

the curtain flickered to the light of the half-burnt lamp, the stillness of the night no relief to either the heat or the feeling of loss that had set in. the thirst set in, unquenchable, then desperation, the craving, finally dissipating into an exhausted sleep.

a sleep full of memories long stored as each emotion cried for completeness, as if the detached need to withdraw was no other than to resurrect the very emotions that had produced the detachment.

yet the memories did not exist in earlier emotional worlds. new emotions emerged as each memory created its own future.

Beginnings

How does one recount the beginning of a journey? Where does it start, and where does it reach its climax? Its incompleteness starts yet another cycle, another threshold to be crossed or attained.

The crossroads become a leitmotif, a symbol that operates and connects at many levels. For me, in this context, it is the intersection of internal and external geographies—between strange, unfinished memories and the uncanny revelations of the present.

Awakening slowly to the dawn sounds of birds after an agitated sleep, a sleep of movement anticipating the shifts and jolts of new travels. No longer the familiar comfort of domesticity, of everyday rhythms; instead the mix of apprehension, agitation and curiosity that accompanies me every time I start a journey, particularly one on which I drive myself. Indian roads are a challenge to everyone, but all the more so for a woman driver, who must negotiate not only the potholes but the hordes of men, all trying to overtake so as to ascertain my gender. I drive unconsorted, a phenomenon of a foreign world. The constant refrain—*Madam, which country?*

The dense fog of the morning adds to the feeling of apprehension. It also defeats the entire purpose of getting up to the dawn light, which today seems hardly visible. The city seems enshrouded in an impenetrable veil of mist and pollution. In all my years of travelling, I have never started on a morning like this. Early-morning winter light has always had for me a sense of wonder, as if with each ray of light, a certain daily mystery reveals itself. I have begun all my previous trips on this light note.

The fog is early this year, unprecedented in its extremity. Stories abound of delayed flights and trains, of cars crashing into headlightless trucks.

I allow myself an extra hour of twilight stupor as I coin this state, neither awake nor asleep, typical of the nether state of in-betweenness. The light filters slowly through the thick white curtain as the jeep winds its way through the dense Delhi traffic.

I make the customary fuel and air stop. I check the air in my tyres extra-carefully, as if sensing the small crisis that awaits us. Sure enough, two hours later, when the jeep is finally out of the extended industrial area and its seemingly unending stream of fumes, I let my concentration waver to the smell of burnt rubber. It is coming from my car. A piece of burning coal has entrenched itself in the tyre groove. The rubber has been slowly burning away, the tyre steadily losing air. It is beyond repair, and there is no shop in this rural vicinity where I can buy a new tyre. It will have to wait till Mathura.

A few minutes later, I am enjoying the clear and relatively smooth highway, savouring the view of the waiting-to-be-harvested wheat fields barely fourteen kilometres from Mathura —just before the little ugly town of Vrindavan, supposedly the birthplace of Krishn, situated on the banks of the sewage canal known as the holy river Yamuna. Suddenly I am in a huge traffic jam, a din of blaring horns, shrill loud-speakers and hysterical screaming voices—a procession to mark the birth of Krishn. A tamasha of overflowing people in tractors, bullock carts, elephants, scooter-rickshaws, tongas, trucks, vans, in fact any kind of believable and unbelievable form of transport. A true representation of neo-Hinduism, celebrating the birth

6

of yet another baby boy. Baby boys are gods, after all, each a potential incarnation of baby Krishn. The jeep inches forward, and in a state of wry cynicism and frayed ears I wonder at my own absurd search and sense of pilgrimage.

Baby Krishn

My memory wanders to another travel experience. I was trying to relocate some sculptures that I had earlier seen outdoors at a site called Budhi Mandu (Ancient Mandu) in Madhya Pradesh. The site had been difficult to access. There had been no paved road and even the kachhi sark (mud path) had only been jeepable up to a point. I had then hired a cycle, but even that took me only so far. I walked the last couple kilometres to find numerous figures strewn along a hill, and, atop the hill, the remnants of a temple city. Rows of sculpture bearing the characteristic Archaeological Survey of India numbering stood in a neat line.

Where was the sculpture now? I enquired of the local people. Did I need to revisit the site, or had it been moved to some museum godown?

Jeep nahin jayegi—bahut barsaat aayi thi. Kachhi sark ka kya kahna? Suna to hai ke murthiyan to sab museum mein hain.

The jeep will not go—the monsoon was too heavy. And who knows what has become of the mud path? We have heard that all the sculptures are in the Dhar museum.

I made my way to Dhar and asked directions to the local museum. I was directed to a bedraggled musty building. The curator-cum-owner greeted me with a burst of unexpected enthusiasm.

Aayai, aayai—ye ghar hamara Madame Tussa jaise hai. Come, come—our house is just like Madame Tussaud's.

Dusty, decrepit, decaying blue-green walls housed a host of famous political figures, the kind of artistic masterpieces that adorn the chowks of small towns. The entire Gandhi family was present in plaster of Paris.

'Come, come, let me show you my masterwork.' The man beckoned me to a little chamber of his own construction, opened the curtain, switched on a light, and lo and behold, there he was—baby Krishn on a swing, with shimmering blue-green-pink lights indicating his divine presence. But the climax was still to come. Another switch was flipped and the swing started to rock and roll to the music of its own little jingle bells.

Look, look how his expression changes—first he is sad, and now so shaitan [mischievous].

Baby Krishn to Kali

'Mama mia, Kali mia—why do you do this to me?' I think as I proceed to the next museum. I find the right museum, but there is no sculpture. I am told to enquire in yet another museum; again no sculpture.

The director proudly informs me, 'Yes, it is all here. The government gave me money to put the sculpture away. Here, see photos. Here is me, and here is my good wife.' Sure enough, they are photographs of the site, but they feature only the man's smiling face and his small, fat, greasy body. It is easy enough to see where the money has gone: into his belly. But the sculptures?

Can I visit the site? I ask.

No problem, Madam. I give you guide.

The guide proves to be as useless as his director. Not only

does he not remember the way, but like all good Indians he will not concede this fact. Eventually I find recourse in my own memory and the familiar landmarks. The strewn sculptures lie exactly as I last saw them. The image that is frozen in my memory lies now before me, unchanged, as if in a timeless zone.

What a strange day—to begin with a baby Krishn doing disco and end with a Kali-shakti pith, resplendent in memory and materiality.

I revert to the road, to the town of Vrindavan. *Vrind* means circle; *van* means forest. Its original fame was not due to its being the birthplace of Baby Krishn but as a Kali-shakti site.

Once upon a time the love of Radha and Krishna was celebrated. Krishna was not a leering Romeo but an avatar of Kali. The two were known then as sakhivallabhis, beloved female friends. Somewhere along the line, the 'a' fell out of Krishna and a chromosome shift took place: XX turned into XY. Baby Krishn was born.

The original myth is still told, but in a somewhat transmuted form.

The local villagers are jealous of Radha and Krishna's illicit love. How can it be? Radha is a married woman, even if she is forever barren. The villagers plot to catch the lovers red-handed. Spies are dispatched to find their hideout. There they are, hand in hand, but to the villagers' dismay, Krishn is a woman! How can two women be lovers? Where is the man?

Delayed starts, a tamasha jam, a burnt tyre . . . I could not have asked for a better beginning. The hysteric procession continues into Mathura.

On this route Mathura's museum has long been my first stop. Housed until recently in an old colonial building, it has one of the best terracotta collections in India, perhaps in the world. It not only smells of decay but *is* in decay. The staff has a totally bored, vacuous look and appears to move as if in slow motion. It's a miracle if the lights function, and the terracotta section is often inexplicably shut; and in any case, for lack of space the main collection is housed in the museum's godowns. Only if one is willing to jump through the hoops of bureaucracy can one access these dark, vaulted chambers. On my last attempt it took me five trips, many pleas, and a few actual pats on my head by the officer in charge to gain entry to three of them—and there are at least thirty more, each overflowing with sculpture, none of which is ever exhibited. According to a leading archaeologist, only that is excavated which fits into the experts' framework. The rest is left underground.

Like Vrindavan and Delhi, Mathura is on the Yamuna and has been home to many civilizations, going back thousands of years. Now only a few traces are visible—some are locked up, some scattered in other museums, many subterranean. The rest have been destroyed by time or invasion.

A La Recherche du Temps Perdu is the title of Marcel Proust's epic novel—recovery of lost time, in search of lost time, researching lost time as a process of memory, a travelogue of memory, a psychoanalysis of memory. But which memory, which reality, which fragment?

I am driving National Highway 3, which goes from Delhi to Mathura to Agra and eventually becomes one of the major arteries to Kanyakumari. It is one of the most crowded highways in India but the surface is fairly smooth, and when I am completely concentrated I can actually cover these two-hundred-odd kilometres in three hours. Excellent time even for a rally driver.

I detest Agra and will make any detour around it. The Taj Mahal is a monument of no vitality—a white elephant that, far from celebrating love, was founded on a culture of violent excess. Mumtaz, to whom it is dedicated, died in her fourteenth childbirth. The architect who built it got paid in true fashion—he had his eyes taken out so he could not construct anything similar. Shah Jahan, the glorious emperor who for his glorious love had the above erection, later paid the same price: his youngest son Aurangzeb had his eyes gouged out and Shah Jahan spent his last years in blind confinement, contemplating, perhaps, his blind lust. Absolute symmetry is the Taj's signature, a symmetry for which every kind of monolithic ideology strives.

I keep driving in this direction, not knowing where I am headed. The road splits, and another turn appears which I have never seen before. The road is smooth as a carpet. The turn leads to a small mound overlooking the river Yamuna, and I am amazed by the clarity of its waters. As I walk down the mound, a temple becomes visible. It is a yogini temple, completely intact, each yogini magnificent in her splendour and detail. So close to Delhi, so easily accessible and yet no one disturbs my contemplation.

I am back on the northeastern part of Delhi's Ring Road. Offices have shut for the day, and the street is filled with crowded buses emitting black soot. I look for a side road that can take me out of this impervious fog. Synchronically I find myself on a quiet secluded path, with not another vehicle or moving object in sight. I have the feeling the path has been

11

created specially for me. It comes to an end. I alight from my jeep to find a little track that descends to the banks of the Yamuna.

I walk down, and to my amazement I see another yogini site, this one not on a mound but hidden in a small ravine. As I climb to the other side, the banks reappear and the river's waters glisten in the red light of dusk.

Many times now have I had these dreams, so vivid that I do not know where the boundary between the reality of the dream and that of awakening lies.

What is this pilgrimage that I began many years ago, knowingly and unknowingly, into this labyrinth of time and memory? Do I look for my reflection, my desired cosmology, as if only in that search do I have a right to live and a right to die?

Bypass

I bypass Mathura, bypass my ritual stop, bypass seeing again the exquisite terracottas—miniscule in size, barely a few centimetres high, yet conveying the expanse of another civilization buried two to five thousand years in linear time. I console myself with my memory of the collection of terracottas from the Ganga and Sindhu valley civilizations in the ethnographic museum in Berlin, their details even finer, displayed in near-perfect light.

I turn off on to the bypass road to Bharatpur. 'Bypass' is a strange concept that has made its way into the vocabulary of many an Indian language. It aptly conveys the desire to avoid the overwhelming crowds of the overgrown villages that form the maddening towns. Roads are sometimes almost non-existent. Water and sewage pipes overflow the narrow lanes on which earlier only bicycles, bullock carts, animals and people would tread instead of trucks, buses, vans, scooters, tempos, cars, jeeps and squatting children who love to run suddenly across. Bypass the shit, bypass the blaring loudspeakers, bypass the shrieking blowing of horns, and above all bypass the people.

The road to Bharatpur, barely thirty kilometres long, is usually so filled with potholes that I count myself lucky if the stretch lasts only an hour. This time it has been repaired, and I am pleasantly astonished to find that the repaired stretch continues to the outskirts of town. I am relieved, as a puncture without a spare tyre would have been catastrophic. I can actually enjoy the country road, the lack of traffic, the brilliant blue of the kingfishers and nilkanth (blue jays) streaking over the fields of corn and wheat.

Bharatpur is known for its bird sanctuary. Every winter, thousands of birds from over a hundred different species migrate here from their colder abodes in China, Central and West Asia, and Europe. They once provided hunting targets for a bored aristocracy. Now, as I sit on a floating boat on the wetlands in the sunset light, I muse that they provide me with a sanctuary, interiority, away from the chaos, suffocation and density of the human world.

Sated by the sounds and sights of birds in golden-red water hues, I venture into the crowded town to look for a spare tyre. So quickly do worlds change in the space of a few kilometres. It is pitch-dark and the streets are unlit, crowded and, as per norm, potholed. I enquire about tyre shops and am considerably advised on a short cut—but the short cut is for a bicycle, pedestrian or perhaps a cow or bullock cart. After an adventurous drive that I would have loved to have bypassed,

13

bumping along Bharatpur's small, dark, very narrow winding streets, descending and ascending into various cavities that encompass practically the breadth of the road, I finally arrive at the intercity bus terminal, around which is the customary row of truck-bus-car mechanics and auto shops. It is past nine p.m. and I am lucky to find any tyre shops open. The jeep makes it to the first one. None of the known brands exist, but copies are sold for half the price, their quality a question of trial and error.

The shop is manned by a fifteen-year-old boy named, like millions of others, Pappu. He is obviously a connoisseur of tyres, and he has learnt to near perfection the art of bargaining. After a playful but very professional negotiation of the tyre price, he curiously asks me, 'Madam, which country?' I reply, continuing in the purest of Sanskritic Hindi, that I am sadly of the same national brand, at which point he laughs and asks me which village I come from. Delhi, I reply. The scale may differ there, but not the density!

I ask him about his job, his ambitions and his formal education. The answer is as expected—he went to school for a while, enough to learn to read a little and sign his name, but, more important, he has a profession. He has already risen, and fast. He informs me with a bright smile that he makes a decent salary—Rs 1,200 a month—and, what's more, he has good prospects. In short, he is happy with his life of spending twelve to fourteen hours per day repairing and selling all kinds of tyres. He knows the brands, the sizes, the kinds of tread, which treads are recyclable, which ones can be used for punctures, how to pad cut tyres or even completely bald ones. I think of a tyre puncture I once experienced in Berlin—repairing it was

14

more expensive then buying a new tyre, equivalent to exactly Pappu's salary. Even in India's major cities this particular art of tyre repair is fast dying; only in small towns and villages does it remain artisanal work. Should I be nostalgic?

I buy a recycled tyre. I have ten thousand kilometres ahead, and I think its quality will be more than adequately tested by the conditions I will traverse. If it gets cut or burnt, I will have lost only half as much money as I would have spent. But the philosophical question always remains: is the short cut, or short price, really better in the long run?

Who knows?! What I do know is that I have a spare tyre again.

Ullu ka Patha

The rickshaw driver in the bird sanctuary shows me two different sets of owls. The sight of owls always has always felt auspicious to me, perhaps because their capacity to see in darkness symbolizes hidden forms of consciousness accessible only through the third eye. Yet in popular consciousness they are to be shunned, and condemned by a curse phrase—*ullu ka patha*, offspring of an owl. The curse has an old history; its traces can be found in the *Rig Ved*. The hero, Indr, is said to have eclipsed the great goddesses and raped Usha, the goddess of dawn and dusk. Yet he remained fearful of the goddesses' powers and the possibility of retribution. They were likened to night birds—they had the powers of both flight and sight, the flight of ecstasy and the sight of the third eye.

A southern legend says: Once upon a time, Shiv asked Kali if he could borrow her third eye. He, too, wanted to be able to glimpse this other world. She willingly lent it to him, but he refused to return it. Once she had lost her power, he could marry and domesticate her.

But the tradition of unconsorted goddesses continues. They are called the matrikas, or mothers, headed by the goddess Chamunda, who rides an owl with a male corpse beneath her. The sons of these matrifocal traditions are called *ullu ka patha*. Bastards, so to speak.

Just as I am quietly relishing my delight at the sight of the owls, a fat deer walks up to us. The driver introduces her as Ramdas, the female deer, and tells me her story. One day, a poor orphaned baby deer came to the sanctuary's local Ram temple. Her parents had been killed by a pack of wild dogs. The young priest was enamoured by her and fed her milk, juice and the choicest of foods until she grew in size. The driver is particularly ironic about the masculine name of the female deer.

Mythologically, the story of Ram and the deer follows a different path. Ram comes to Sri Lanka as a king in exile. He is offered hospitality by Lanka's king, Ravan. Women move about freely, voluptuously. The ravishing sister of Ravan, originally named Suparnarekha—beautiful golden wings, their line, their flight—greets Ram's brother Lakshman lewdly. This merits a castrating punishment, and in a rage Lakshman cuts off her nose. Ravan is furious, and seduces Ram into the forest by shamanizing himself into a magical deer. Ram tests all of his skills to hunt and ensnare the deer, but to no avail. He is so lost in pursuit that he loses all sense of time. Meanwhile, he has left his virginal wife Sita in the tutelage of Lakshman. When Lakshman leaves to search for Ram, he draws a line around Sita—his signature, the lakshman-rekha. But Ravan is an alchemical trickster, capable of donning many forms. He becomes a pure ascetic Brahmin and demands that Sita fulfil her caste duty by stepping over the line and giving him his due. Abduction occurs. Is it an act of freedom?

Ravan was so gifted that the gods granted him a boon: he asked that he not be killed by divine forces, but that he forget the mortal world and its treachery. Ram, of course, was the ultimate male hero of this world, having conquered his fate through betrayal; thus did Ram claim godhood. He never had children of his own, and Lakshman always lived close to him. Sita remained virginal not only in his company, but also during the time she spent with Ravan. Only when she was later exiled did she parthenogenically produce two male twins. Sita herself was born from the earth. Etymologically, her name means *cleft*: vagina of the earth. The tradition independent of her alliance with Ram sees her as an agricultural goddess who stood for a social system in which women tilled and inherited the land.

But now, in Bharatpur, I am faced with a cute, fat, spoilt female dear—sublimated as Ram's male servant. Authentic sexuality is best left open to speculation.

Nowhere do the wondrous and the absurd intersect as in contemporary India.

Red Roses and Fortification

The princely city of Gwalior is my next stop. I decide against bypassing Agra, as the 'short cut' saves kilometres but not necessarily energy or time. Fifty kilometres of bad road is worse than three hundred kilometres of good road if it leaves the body and nerves in a state of rattled shock. After completing one such journey, I opened the bag where I keep a torch, and to my shock the entire torch had come apart. Another time, I

17

suddenly felt a gush of cold wind streaming into the jeep—the back latch was merrily swinging in the air. All the nuts and bolts had gone with the wind and the rattling roads. The road through Agra is a carpet in comparison.

But this means driving through the most crowded part of the medieval city. There is no secret path to circumvent the narrow lanes that the highway suddenly breaks into. The roads have been widened, but they are still not constructed for problem-free traffic. Manoeuvring through the pigs, stray dogs, cows, buffaloes, goats, piles of excrement, bicycles four abreast, trucks unloading and reversing into the incoming traffic, blaring horns, peddlers selling their wares and beggars trying to bless me with baby sons . . . nightmare of all nightmares, I finally reach the outskirts of the city and am on National Highway 3 again. A distance of perhaps five kilometres took a little less than an hour.

A sense of relief floods through me. The most difficult part of the drive is over, and I can savour the rest of the hundred kilometres of smooth highway that makes its way through the huge bridge that overlooks the river Chambal and the surrounding ravines. A spectacular landscape announces one's arrival into Madhya Pradesh from Rajasthan or Uttar Pradesh. What are these demarcations between the different states? How were they set up—what is the role of colonial history, the role of modern India as an independent nation-state?

But my research is that of an older history, an age bypassed by recent epochs. The ravines that are famous today as the former abode of Phoolan Devi were once, a thousand years ago, part of a network of yogini sites. I have visited three—but how many more were there?

I arrive in the newer part of Gwalior, where large roads await me. The route to the hotel is uncomplicated and I know it well. The hardest part of long-distance driving is arriving in a crowded city and not knowing where to go. Maps do not exist, and when they do they are usually inaccurate. The best way to find a place is still to ask a couple of people and put faith in the majority answer—and not in words but in gestures. It took me many years of travel in India to realize that most people do not have the concept of journeying to new places to explore them. Life exists in a closed area, confined to domesticity. Its lakshman-rekha is not to be traversed, the beyond (the Sanskrit *para*) not to be explored. How, then, can one fit into the traveller's shoes? Travel is undertaken for social reasons or sheer necessity. Traditionally the 'mystic' wanderer was the social exception, the uncontrolled periphery, and meetings with 'him' had to be kept within contained boundaries.

Arriving at the hotel is pleasant. I am a regular visitor here, and the staff and the waiters know me well. Madhya Pradesh is the only state with a tourism department that works, somewhat, and unlike most government hotels, this one employs a woman at reception. The hotel was built more than twenty years ago in what was then a quiet area; today the silence is often broken by marriage processions composed of people who seem to believe they have to overcompensate for the empty jar of arranged-marriage mediocrity by blaring their bandbaaja. Romantic loss? Civilizational loss?

My mind harkens back to an image found in Sanskrit love poetry: lovers so enraptured in each other's gazes, so silent in their contemplation of each other, that even the peacocks do not shy from grazing around them.

I grew up with the presence of peacocks. How many times have I seen them perched on the terraces of Delhi? On how many drives have I been blessed by the performance of their dance? They used to be a natural phenomenon in Indian cities, but now they are a dwindling species.

The hotel has some kind of vision despite its peeling paint, and the garden still has its charm. Climbing bougainvillea has now ascended past the building's two floors. It is still too early for the dahlias and hibiscus, but some roses are apparent—Indian roses of brilliant red, unmistakable in their fragrance. Like bougainvillea and hibiscus, they can withstand excruciating summer heat.

I grew up with roses of all colours, all shapes, and all fragrances. A hundred-odd roses grew in my father's factory, and I developed a capacity to identify each one purely through its odour. The factory and roses represented the Nehruvian dream of combining industrialization with romantic aesthetics, in this case the *gul* of Urdu ghazals.

My father could not decide whether to be a painter or an engineer. He chose to design machinery and grow roses. Half his factory land became a gulistan in which the entire family passionately participated.

The factory did not take long to die. The paradise of roses became a chimera, and my father lost himself to the excessive pleasures of alcohol, but my sense of fragrance remains. A red rose in the mouth, expressing a current of desire that could flood through any dam, break any closet door—is that, too, a declining species? A vestige of the last decadents, or as hardy as the red Indian rose?

Sitting out in the heat of the winter sun, sipping the

customary cup of spiced ginger tea after the morning drive, I think about the hotel's architecture. An inner courtyard, an outer garden and terrace and a curving balcony wrapping around the rooms combine for a curious blend of the inner and the outer. There is solar heating for the hot water. Apparently designed for the weary traveller, the place is surprisingly sensitive to the aesthetics of a certain meditative calm.

After a brief afternoon rest, my timing is on schedule. I drive up to the hill where the old temples stand. Today the hill is known not for its temples but for its medieval fort and palace.

Forts are a medieval phenomenon. There seems to have been no fortressing of these hill sites prior to the Islamic invasions; there are no apparent remnants of civic, political or royal architecture from before the thirteenth century. In other ways, however, this hill bears witness to at least two thousand years of history. Old temples, sculptures in caves, the medieval Mansingh palace (which changed hands many times between Rajput and Mughal rulers), an English military base, the princely Scindia school and a towering white gurdwara are all contained within the crumbling fortress walls.

Gwalior's hill was more often than not a cosmological site. It was the climax of a pilgrimage to the openness of the sky, a space apart from the villages and cultivated fields on the plains below. It was a space for contemplation, a place to gaze upon the life that throbbed below. Even today the view from the top is spectacular, with the different parts of the city visible in their different historicities—the green zones, the modern city and the crowded medieval areas that lie at its feet.

Fortressing the hill led to the palace becoming a symbol of royal and military power, something to be violently fought over. The Mughal prince Murad found refuge in the Rajput king Mansingh's abode. When Murad's younger brother Aurangzeb conquered the palace, however, he executed his elder here. What was once Murad's sanctuary became his dungeon, his death grounds. Blood spilt over the hillsides as elephants trampled the strewn corpses.

I drive through the crowded galis, now surprisingly cleaner, more organized. The city has had the good sense to make some of the lanes one-way. I usually get lost in these winding lanes, which seem to represent the intricate labyrinth of life. There are no straight lines, only curving paths that seem to lead nowhere, and trying to reverse the jeep on these dead-end roads can be a nerve-racking task. By this time I have learnt to look out for the single-gauge rail track that the English built to take them to their hilltop destiny—it now lies in disuse but the corresponding footpath remains, and of course the old elephant track, used by motor vehicles now. The ascent is steep, and a radio signal monitors the flow of traffic in only one direction.

The late-afternoon light glows on the red sandstone of the temples. Traces of destruction, vandalism, natural decay and manipulative reconstruction are evident in the temples' histories. The Islamic invasions left their imprints on the sculptures: their faces are viciously disfigured, as Allah may not be depicted in the human form, particularly the feminine. Does this harken back to the destruction of the earlier goddesses Hind, Manat, Al-uzza and Al-lat of central and western Asia? Did Islam smash these divinities the way Indr raped Usha? Was not Al-lat, the epitome of the 'seductive evil' goddess, representative of

22

the 'decadent' Arab world that Mohammad sought to replace? With one consonant shift, a new faith was established.

Traces of war and of the colonization of sacred spaces are as present in the temples as their original architectural and spacial principles. The temple is constructed as an octagon: two squares that intersect so that the lines connecting their corners form eight equilateral triangles. The stone is still, yet these graphics allude to the notion of harmonically moving squares with one focal point. At one time, they constellated a circle in which the centre was not fixed, and the space between each of the eight pillars was not barricaded. Open in both directions, the network of empty passages accentuated the play of light.

Light no longer flows. A 'central' sanctum was added by the British, with all best intentions, and the Archaeological Survey of India has retained this blatant discrepancy. Ironically, then, the sanctum lies outside the original space of the temple, but has become the dominant paradigm of the 'Hindu' temple. It is now the central chamber that must be occupied. The architectural womb, *garbh grih*, must procreate a male child-god.

The intricacy of the sculptural engraving is in sharp counterpoint to the attempts to destroy it. Even the attempt to erect the central womb appears absurd; it seems a lifeless prison cell, its door kept permanently closed by a huge padlock. The god that should have graced its presence is conspicuous—in his absence. Perhaps he needed his freedom.

What was so fearful in these delicate carvings that they merited such violence? And what is so terrifying in not having a centre to which all must be subordinated?

23

In the surviving stone remnants, the dancing figures possess an even greater grace as their faces bear witness to overwhelming brutality. The more I see their fine lines, the less I seem to see their mutilation—as if I must, somewhere, through an inner gaze, be able to see them whole again, unlike the blank absence of either Allah or the supposed Vishnu locked up in his cell.

The doorway to this cell has carvings of the unconsorted goddesses, the matrikas.

Matrika
ma = matrix, creative principle
tri = three
ika = the feminine ending

Contained in the name is the dynamic philosophy of the recurring three, a numerology outside the confines of duality. In their polyphonic exuberance, the matrikas are their own dancing peripheries.

With a kinship system of multiple mothers, the matrikas overflow the boundaries of constricted fiefdom. Their chain of life and death is interchanging. The child becomes the corpse; the mothers that give life also take it back. The womb is both fecund and barren.

Vinayak

Ullu ka pathas abound here, as at most temples sites where panels depict matrikas with them. They are said to be vinayak (*vin* = without, *nayak* = male). They are the original celestial musicians, the laughing Buddhas and the shamans. They are the guardians of doorways and thresholds. They invite; they initiate. They can also block entry.

The goddess Parvati is enjoying herself in pleasurable waters with her female companions. She does not want their privacy disturbed by some intrusive male god, so out of her own bodily fluid (*mal*) she creates a handsome and charming man to stand as her doorkeeper and block men from entering. The god Shiv tries to defy this barrier. In sheer rage at being denied entry, he beheads the charming young man.

Parvati emerges in rage, transforms herself into a wrathful Kali, and Shiv trembles like a terrified child. To appease her, he cuts the head of the first passerby he sees—an elephant—and sets it on the body of the young man. Ganesh.

In another story, Parvati is standing on the banks of the Ganga. She bends down and drinks the waters that carry the elephant-woman's *mal*, and lo and behold she is pregnant with Ganesh.

The elephant head represents both memory and the matriarchy of the animal world. One of the names of the elephant-headed woman/devi was Matangi (*mata* = matrix, mother, *angi* = part). Another name was Malini, derived from *mal*, the feminine fluid through which parthenogenesis could take place.

In these two matrika panels, the elephant-headed figure is feminine. This iconography appears to be older than its masculine afterthought. It is embodied in a two-thousand-year-old terracotta sitting somewhere in the Mathura godowns.

As I slowly descend the steep slope, niches appear in the hill wall. A massive matrika in a reclining position majestically appears in the light of the setting sun. Its size and iconography date it between the first and fourth centuries. Contrasting temporal periods, contrasting cosmogonies, civilizations, all expressed through memories in stone. In another niche another manipulation is visible: the main figure has been hacked out and replaced by a Jain sculpture. The smaller figures are, again, two matrikas.

So present, so revered, so feared and yet so desecrated—is that the space these matrikas occupy in today's consciousness? Or are they, like me, asked, *Madam, which country?*

I have not seen the customary vultures, one of the birds associated with matrikas, sitting on their temple perch or on the fort walls. They, too, are feared, a fear I have never managed to comprehend. They eat the dead, after all, not the living.

Museums

The next morning I go to the base of the Gwalior hill, where the medieval palace has been turned into a museum. It is ten a.m., but there is no one at the ticket office. I go up the narrow stairs into the courtyard, where the museum workers are sunning themselves. They know me well by now and leave me to my solitude. The small rooms that were once the abode of the princely aristocracy, whether Rajput or Mughal, now contain some of the best surviving sculptures from earlier temples. They are neatly divided by epoch and gender. The rooms rarely have light, but the sculptures are well sheltered. A few other pieces of assorted unsorted sculpture stand in the sunlit courtyard. It is a curious ad-hoc arrangement, an amalgam that reflects a peculiar aesthetics of blending histories, blurring time zones.

What are museums if not storehouses of memories, of artefacts uprooted from their original contexts? And is this not the nature of time, its tides, its ebbs and flows? Is this not the human experience of time: the accumulation of memories? Is this not time's greatest mystery—that which lives on despite many deaths, that which survives as time's traces and unfinished memories? Are museums, then, places to muse and meditate on these memories?

A journey into old temple histories is intricately connected to the quality of museum visits. What is collected? What is displayed? What is locked up in the godowns of bureaucracy? What treasure does one suddenly discover? What is one's darshan, what is one's perception?

One of my most notable visits was the museum of Indore. I arrived in Indore to find that the government guest house was full. As I could not afford a hotel, I thought I would just visit the museum and drive on. At the museum I asked to meet the curator, Mr Garg, and he was intrigued by my search. He told me about two sites, Budhi Mandu and a goddess temple in Ali Rajpur, and showed me several photographs detailing the different findings. There were no pictures of him or his family. But it would be a long drive, he suggested; it would be more feasible to stay the night in Indore. He offered me one of the offices as a guest room—the long table could serve as my bed—and I readily accepted. After spending the day photographing and musing on the museum's collection, I slept in its atmosphere.

The next day I left for Budhi Mandu. I asked the villagers near the site if they knew the way. All I got in reply were garbled mutterings, the gist of which was that I should go to (new) Mandu.

Hilltop Mandu is a well-known tourist destination, famous for its fifteenth-century Islamic romantic palace, which was specially designed as a place for the king and his special wife to escape the summer heat. Mr Garg had told me that Mandu now had a makeshift museum, and that I could probably find a guide there to take me to the site. I could also see some of the findings they had managed to transport.

The makeshift museum turned out to be a dimly lit godown in which the caretaker lived. A camp cot, a small kerosene stove and a few pieces of clothing gave the sculptures some surreal embellishment.

The caretaker had never been to Budhi Mandu but promptly offered to take me there. The distance of twenty-five kilometres, which we covered partly in the truck, partly on hired cycles and partly on foot, took six hours.

Ruined temples and sculptures were everywhere. It was as if this innocuous mount concealed another epoch of history, an expansive citadel long obliterated by its well-known counterpart.

At the end of the day I was in the same position the caretaker was—no place to stay except the godown. I was invited to use it as a night halt.

It is only in some of these MP museums that I have had pleasant experiences, only in MP that there is still sometimes an unconscious or even conscious dignity about the civilizational wealth of the past.

Kota, in Rajasthan not far from the MP border, was the polar opposite. The archaeological museum opened two hours late, a regular practice for which no excuse was needed. Photography was not allowed, the museum official spouted gleefully.

Where could I get permission? I asked.

Go to Jaipur, I was told. Jaipur is only 280 kilometres away.

The state of the museum was pitiful. The sculptures were not even dated, and there was no information on where they had been found. A dust-covered map of the neighbouring localities hung in one corner, so I asked the official for a piece of paper to note down the sites.

Writing is not allowed, he spitefully reiterated. Get permission from Jaipur.

Archaeological museums, like much else in India, have predominantly male curators. One exception was in Vidisha, a small town in Madhya Pradesh—the only woman curator I have met in fifteen years of visiting Indian archaeological museums. She was warm and friendly, shared all the information she had, showed me the entire collection and gave me excellent road instructions. Ten years later I was in the local museum at Hoshangabad, three hundred kilometres from Vidisha, and found to my surprise that she had been transferred there. She recognized me, offered me tea, opened all the rooms and even showed me the hidden or 'reserved' parts of the collection.

I was touched that she had remembered me. Then again, how could she forget me—a woman alone, driving a small truck? It turned out that she had narrated our meeting to anyone who would hear it, particularly her daughter. She told me proudly that her daughter now lives independently.

For many, museums are dead space, an invention of the colonial imagination, a recent hangover. What is the point of collecting stone? What is the point of spending resources to transport and preserve? What a job it is lugging these heavy sculptures from remote places in some jungle or the other! And what relevance has this history to us? These views are expressed by bureaucrats, historians and intellectuals alike.

Living temples are often their preference. These temples generate income, provide a thriving, tax-free economy and are living tamasha at its theatrical best.

A few years ago, in Delhi, I woke up at the crack of dawn to a loudspeaker order to give milk to the god Ganesh. One would be blessed, one was told, if he drank the milk and cursed if he did not. Crowds thronged to any temple they could find; queues formed outside the cow sellers' doors. Milk was spilt in abundance on dirty temple floors as the bare- and sticky-footed crowd tried everything to make Ganesh drink his milk. If one let one's neighbour know that one's milk had been refused, all the sins tucked away in safe closets would spill out.

Cow sellers mixed water in the milk to increase their profits while temple priests used every psychological ruse to milk their unending clients. People who had never visited temples in their lives suddenly developed intense religious inclinations. The loudspeakers provided a running commentary of Ganesh's antics. This phenomenon was orchestrated not only all over India but also in faraway lands—many 'lost' NRIs and even some ABCDs rushed to reclaim their Hindu identity by giving Ganesh his milk. Hinduism had finally come of age.

I am biased, no doubt, being perhaps one of the few people on earth who did not have the joy of her mother's milk. There was no gender discrimination there; my brother, too, was brought up on milk powder, unlike the millions of baby Krishns who continue their breast addiction till age five and beyond. We did not, however, escape the middle-class (and all else who could afford it) regime of hot milk three times a day. So began and ended my day, with this trauma of drinking hot milk with the fat intact.

My worst memory is that of being delivered back to my house from nursery school when I was three. I was crouched on the front of the cycle bar when a car appeared from nowhere. The gallant cycle driver jumped off and I fell like a sack of potatoes, the cycle crashing over me. There was no major damage to the cycle or me, apart from a bleeding nose, and an elderly family took me in. Thinking I was in shock, they insisted I drink hot milk. Wonderful shock treatment—having to drink hot milk for the fourth time in one day.

The yoginis do not believe in drinking milk. They drink blood, the elixir of life, and it is this wine on which they get drunk.

After Gwalior's museum I head towards one of the yogini sites, about fifteen kilometres away. Most of the important sculptural findings have been transferred to the palace museum, and some of the best pieces—despite the illegality of taking pieces over a hundred years old out of the country—are in an American museum. Yet not one of the sculptures is completely intact. Many are beheaded, some are disfigured and some have had their breasts, arms or legs brutally hacked. The violence is a given, its terrorism blatant, but survival has its own special revelations.

Who were, and who are, the yoginis?

yog =	fusion	
ini =	feminine ending	
yoni =	vulva, origin, waterfall, cave, source	

A forgotten cosmology, a lost matriarchy, exquisitely unbelievable mythologies, magical wondrous female figures that could supposedly take any form, any size, any weight.

31

Flying through time and space, they could suddenly manifest themselves and then, equally suddenly, become invisible. Yet the popular tradition fears them. They represent the ultimate femme fatale, able to consume a person with their all-powerful sexuality, to swallow him or her with a snap of their fingers, their lolling tongues coloured brilliant blood-red.

As in any cosmology, meanings vary according to the interpretative voice and gaze. However, if one navigates the largely untranslated shaktic Sanskrit literature, the myths that abound are variations on one theme. The goddess is away in her ashram-retreat, immersed in her meditation, surrounded by attractive women. She is a kumari (unconsorted) in her dark Krishna avatar. The most powerful male god-demon, Mahesh-asur (*mahesh* = maha, great, *ish* = god, *asur* = demon), asks her hand in marriage. She replies that he must first defeat her in battle.

The male god-demon received special powers when he was parthenogenically born from the matrika called Mahisha (the great goddess), hence his name, Mahesh (the great god). He can regenerate himself each time his blood falls on the earth. A great war takes place, and each battle is won by the kumari as Maheshasurmardini (the killer of Maheshasur), along with her band of yoginis—who drink Mahesh's blood just before it touches the earth. A grand festival of intoxication takes place. Mahesh lies, in fulfilment of his deepest wish, under Kali's feet as a corpse.

The *Yogini Tantra* says:

Once upon a time, there were only the male god and the female goddess. The god decided to challenge the goddess to war in order to see whether his capacity for fission was greater than her capacity for fusion. The goddess replied that without her, the male was equivalent to a corpse.

The god split into a schizophrenic duality, a frenzied destructive deity in which the alter ego lies inert in the feminine expanse. He attains consciousness of the primal Kali form:

Of the dark/black (Krishna) colour, she, the extremely fierce,

Bedecked with a garland of skulls, playing erotically with the serpentess Vali,

Her hair free—glowing radiantly.

The tongue of the universe, three blood fierce eyes, gleaming

With strength and art, the crown emitting scorching heat.

Subsequently, he sees the following vision of the yoginis being born:

In the thousands of (the goddess) Shiva's caves is the potential of the tej mandal (circular ring of intense heat)

The streaming light/heat/blood [maharava] in all four directions creating the cycle of the fierce beyond

Fusing and emerging from the circle of light-rays are the yoginis in each cave

Thus (are born) the yoginis of fierce form, desirous of the great war

from the shadow [pratilom] of the well, the primal egg in the middle of each cave

Illuminating always the goddess of all (forms), the primal Suryi-maya

The mere sight of the above, characterized as the constellation of the mouth [mukh-mandal], sends Mahesh into a faint. The war is over in an instant. Kali swallows him with a flick of the tongue.

Through the lolling tongue, Kali finishes the war.

The mother, along with the primal egg, causing death in a moment.

Poor thing, she did not realize she was standing on her husband! Upon realization, she stuck out her lolling tongue in shame—in compliance.

The story is rarely narrated and remains untranslated. Amnesia creates a modern version.

K(a) is the first consonant in the Sanskrit alphabet. The string of names associated with Kali inevitably contains Kumari and Krishna: a blend of the dark, the wild, the untamed and the unconsorted. *Kali* itself is derived from *karali* (tongue, flame) and the root *kal* (time, darkness). The Sanskrit word for 'vowel' was *matrika*. Here, the matrika 'i' as the ending of Kali represents prototypical feminine energy. The name itself contains the masculine and neuter name Kal—but the reverse is never the case. In the above myth, there is an etymological play on the matrika/vowel 'i'. The goddess tells the male god (Shiv) that he is a corpse—*sh(a)v*—without her, without the matrika 'i'. The goddess herself is named Shiva. This includes the name Shiv, but the inverse is impossible: *Shiv* cannot contain *Shiva*.

Likewise, there is the nomination of the goddess Suryi-maya. *Sury* is the name of the male sun god; Suryi is the generic feminine. Maya, from the root *ma*—to create—connotes the creative magical principal.

34

Feminine	Masculine
Kali	Kal (without matrika/vowel 'i')
Shiva	Shiv (sh(a)v—corpse—without *a*)
Krishna	Krishn
Suryi	Sury
Mahesha	Mahesh
Kumari	Kumar

As I drive towards the site, pondering these names and etymologies, I suddenly realize their inherent linguistic power. Sculptures can be smashed, myths can be manipulated, but the moment one knows their key names and the roots of these names, no amount of linguistic surgery has any relevance. Perhaps that is why one of the principal ways of passing on these cosmological traditions was through the recitation of multiple names, the *sahasr namvalis* (strings of a thousand names). Based on key phonetic roots, the names form the tradition's linguistic iconography, its archi-text-ure.

Names have always fascinated me: giving someone a name, changing one's name, secret names, discovering the enfolding-encoding of a name's symbolic potential. In Sanskrit, things have no fixed words or gender; the poesis lies in how one nominates them. Thus the sun can be called 'dead egg' (martand, *mart* = dead, *and* = egg), whereas from the feminine perspective she can be Suryamayi or Ushas, the glowing one.

Naming is a curious phenomenon—a bestowing of identity, an act of recognition. When a baby is yet unnamed, its identity has yet to be revealed. I try to explain my nameless birth certificate to a German bureaucrat.

He replies: The baby must have a name when it is born,

otherwise the hospital picks an initial letter and gives its own name. Petra or Peter, for example.

Mass common names, particularly pet names, are a phenomenon everywhere. Once a Punjabi family named their three daughters Sweetie, Beauty and Cutey. Must every mass culture erase the particular, exorcise the mystery of naming, the possibility of secret divining? Must identity be a given, controlled at all costs except perhaps in the abysses of one's unconscious?

Secret names, secret desires: A young, beautiful woman from a poor family of daughters got a marriage offer from a rich suitor. She was secretly in love with his brother's wife. The couple got married in the traditional way, wherein the bride gives up her first name as well as her surname. An initial letter was chosen for her. Without realizing it, she took the same name as that of her brother-in-law's wife. Later they became secret lovers.

The blasting of horns ends my reverie. My concentration rivets again to the road. Again I look for the narrow-gauge rail line as my pathfinder, as it runs parallel to the Etawah highway to Naresar.

The first time I took this road, in 1989, I was on the back of a two-wheeler, a Vespa scooter. I had been looking for the yogini sites of Naresar and Mitavali, and it was like looking for a needle in a haystack. No one had heard of either one. I then visited both archaeological museums and hit an apparent jackpot: a young woman working in one museum had heard of the sites. She was excited about visiting them, but unsure of their location. She promised me she would arrive punctually at my hotel the next day at seven a.m.

Seven a.m. came and went, as did eight. Indian time is

stretchable, after all, but I was not sure what to do. I had been on the road for five weeks. My shoestring budget was on its last threads and I had to clear my heavily subsidized room before the next bureaucrat arrived. At ten o'clock, I loaded my luggage into my truck, ready to take my last chance to find these sites. Just then a scooter arrived: my friend from the museum had kept her word. She had found someone who was familiar with one of the villages neighbouring the site and asked him to drive us there, as the rough road would not take my little truck.

After five weeks of travelling completely alone, two companions equally eager to explore historical legacies (not to mention share responsibilities) were a gift. The tarmac on the highway was new, there was hardly any traffic, the weather was perfect—a typically sunny winter day—and the light was just right for photography.

After ten kilometres we stopped to get tea, as we would find no other tea stall on our route. We soon came to the turn-off for the ravine area. The beginnings of a few factories were visible, but otherwise there was a feeling of spatial wilderness, of expansiveness outlined by ravines.

The road slowly disintegrated into pieces of stone. Our driver insisted on trying to drive us through, but we jumped off. It was bad enough for one person to attempt the stones; with the added weight of two other people, we'd been pushing towards a collapse. Walking was a relief compared to the painful bouncing of the scooter.

The first traces of the earlier temple cities became visible—broken pieces of sculpture and stone lay across our path. Each piece of stone was a discovery. What would it lead us to? Our first site was a thousand-year-old round stepwell, elegant and minimal in its perfect circularity. Descending into the earth, it was an architectural metaphor for the yoni, and suddenly the association became myth and architecture became apparent. Sita was supposedly born from the vagina of the earth; had it not been from the waters of a stepwell?

One cannot reduce cosmological metaphors to mere practical realities, yet cosmological spaces did have practical relevance. Here they stored and provided water, rain water and ground water.

After a few more kilometres, we arrived at Bhakteshwar and found a small temple open on all four sides, each representing a different spectrum of divinities. One side had a completely feminine constellation, another side a masculine one, the third a convergence of the feminine and masculine, and the fourth a matrika constellation. A recently constructed wall partially blocked one side but did not completely obscure the original aesthetics.

A few kilometres further were the ruins of another temple city. But we still had not reached our destination, the Mitavali yogini temple. We trekked back towards Bhakteshwar, walked another few kilometres, and gradually, on a faraway hill, a round temple became visible. We exchanged looks in enthralled silence. We meandered around the fields, losing our way a couple of times, and finally arrived at the base of the hill. A flight of stairs awaited us, and though we had already walked over fifteen kilometres and not eaten anything since we had left at ten a.m. neither of us was tired. It was about four in the afternoon when we finally climbed up.

It was an amazing feeling to actually be in the temple, even though the original 'free' centre had again been taken over. A stone lingam had recently been cemented there.

There were no sculptures left, only empty niches and shrines, but it did not matter; there was only the feeling of expansiveness, the feeling of unfolding landscapes, open fields. This hill had not been fortressed. The round, roofless, open-air temple blended into the landscape the way the round stepwell had blended into the earth. The architectural principles were similar, as though linked by a cosmological thread. The openness of the temple on the hill pointed towards the sky, whereas the stepwell pointed in the other direction—underground.

By the time we returned to the main road, the sun had set and the light was fast disappearing. Our driver was too exhausted to drive, and readily turned over his scooter to me. Upon reaching my truck at the guest house, I was told that both rooms were full. I would have to drive at least sixty kilometres, in the dark, to the next town to try my luck at finding discounted accommodation. The Naresar site would have to wait for another trip. We had been told of its existence, but its location was still elusive.

The quality of the road has held, though the traffic has multiplied by leaps and bounds. There is an air-force base on this road, a huge industrial area and two modern masterpieces of ugliness: contemporary temples. The new factories have attracted migrant workers from neighbouring states. Migrant-run dhabhas are everywhere, catering to a permanent bustle of workers and truckers. The side road, which was nothing but holes and stone, has been replaced by an industrial road with a tarmac surface. It is poor in quality, jeepable but not shock-proof. Ten years ago the journey from Gwalior to the Mitavali temple took the entire day; now it takes an hour-and-a-half.

We used to walk about twenty kilometres from the road; now we walk about five.

But this experience of the temple was far from wondrous. In addition to the lingam in the centre, pieces of earlier pillars had been polished and inserted into the yogini shrines. These symbolize the phallus, of course, and the local priest told us this was a Ram temple. He had never heard of the yoginis. The blue board, that hallmark of protected archaeological sites, clearly states at the entrance that any tampering with protected monuments is a crime punishable by prison and fine; but perhaps that, too, is a colonial legacy, not part of the cult of recent Hinduism.

My memories go back and forth between the times I have been on this road. What is this memoric time? What is its chronology? Linear or cumulative? Or cumulative which includes the linear? Has a decade gone by so fast? Has my life changed the way this road has? Do I not expect time to somehow stand still for me, particularly time in India? Have I become like the European visitor, nostalgic for a changeless archaic past? Do I hanker for the ruins of a lost civilization to remain constant, at least in my own memory and its traces? Or do I just feel, at a gut level, the violation of my cosmological sexuality being raped?

Do my memories shuttle back and forth, the way I shuttled back and forth seven years ago on this road, looking for Naresar? I had left early in the morning with my then companion, hoping to show her Mitavali and find Naresar as well. Back and forth we went, asking and asking, but no one in the vicinity had heard of the site. They were, after all, migrant workers, and old temple sites were as far from their consciousness as I was. But a few seemed intrigued, and suggested I try someone local. I went to numerous shops, tea stalls and roadside cafes with the same result: all the proprietors were migrants, and the only temples they could suggest were the ugly modern masterpieces.

Finally, I did find someone local in a village. A young boy took us to a field where we could park the jeep. We crossed a couple of fields and walked up the winding ravines to a hilltop. From there we could see the outline of Mitavali's yogini temple, and hidden inside the ravine was Naresar. We descended to a little shrine with two goddesses engraved on each portal— the customary river goddesses. Inside was an open stone yoni.

A little further on was a small lake surrounded by small shrines. These were empty. One of the sculptures I had seen in the Gwalior palace museum might have belonged here, but I could only be relieved that they were safe—in another temple further up this hill, Chamunda had been beheaded, mutilated, painted and covered with a shimmering red cloth. This was an act of the local villagers, a testimony to their living faith. How could one leave a nude goddess uncovered? After all, the local women must cover their heads in deference; should not their older stone counterparts do the same?

Once in a small village in Orissa, at least two thousand kilometres from where I stood now, I visited two temples dedicated to the twin goddesses Tara and Tarini. Each had her own shrine at a different height on the riverbank. I took the red veil, the ghunghat, off her so I could see what lay beneath and perhaps photograph her. The priest stalked out, ready to strike.

Unfortunately for him, I was already in a rage that had been cooking the entire morning. I had already visited two sites. One was another twin-goddess temple to Tara-Tarini, whose main iconography was an image of two women embracing. This image was now gone, replaced by a heterosexual couple. The second site, Tapta Pani (Steaming Waters), was known for its hot sulphur springs and an old Devi temple. Men were bathing in the steaming springs, and these were channelled into a little cell where women were allowed to bathe. In short, the women were given 'used' waters. I promptly went to the springs, took my clothes off and had my hot bath. The men were too ashamed to look, while the women wore looks of pride and envy.

The appropriation and heterosexualization of the goddess sites and the channelling of the 'leftovers' to the women had prepared me for war. I went for the priest's collar. I hollered in his ears that I was a living Kali, and by her living wrath, how dare he cover my cosmic reflection? He backed off, and I photographed a black figure smeared with oil and incense soot, in a state of near disintegration. Disgusted, I said: This is your veneration, covering up your desecration? The sculptures were made uncovered. How dare you conceal them?

But we have to cover up our women, he said. The time when the sculptures were made was the time of the demons (Rakshas ka zamana tha).

The word *rakshas* comes from *raksha*—to protect. How did the word itself become demonized? And what *is* this phenomenon of demonization, of Othering that is so prevalent at so many social and cultural levels, not to speak of the religious?

I have been collecting stories of demonization, but one is a jewel. I was doing a workshop in the Himalayas with a group of local women on the demonization of the yogini-feminine and the witch-hunting that takes place in many villages. With smiling, twinkling eyes, a woman told this story:

A young man was hopelessly sick, possessed by the dakinis (another yogini epithet). He dreamt of beautiful young women at the pinnacle of their sexuality, capturing him with their seductive threads, tying him up and locking him in an old cave. He was so afraid that he could not leave his room. He asked the woman for her advice. She replied: The next time they come to you, give them a resounding slap on the face and you will be free from their maya. The young man summoned up all his courage, and the next time the dakinis crept up to him he gave them a cracking slap across the face—only to find that he'd slapped his own face.

But neither then nor now do *I* want to be freed from their maya, or break this spell of fascination. I only want to continue on this labyrinthine journey and not lose my path.

The weather was ominous. Clouds had started to gather, and the warm sunlight I had experienced in the courtyards of the palace museum was hiding behind the clouds. Rain is not the norm during winter, particularly on the northern plains. In the last seven years I have been to Naresar five times, and each time I have been blessed with perfect weather and light. Each time I have been able to explore the site further. A year ago I took a group of four women here, and we were completely alone and at peace. Even the cowherds and the ogling boys from a neighbouring village did not break that.

We walked down to the end of the ravine and found a small clearing with broken pieces of stone. It seemed to have been another yogini temple; there were shrines everywhere. At the end of the clearing, an old banyan tree grew out of the remains of an earlier round stepwell. A little further on was another lake. This must have been an oasis of multiple delights.

Over a thousand years later, it was as if I could still be intoxicated by the tranquillity and protectiveness of this enclosed yet open valley. The sun slowly starts descending, and its light changes the gorges' colours to a golden red, blending them into the sandstone remains. No wonder the earlier name for the sun was Ushas—from *ush*, to glow.

Each cosmology has its own aesthetics of light.

This time the light is absent. The group of young boys that has persistently followed me is intent on foiling my experience of the valley's serene pleasures. The gorges are no longer radiant in the light of Ushas, and the habitual circular flight of the vultures and eagles appears ominous, as if transmitting a message in semaphore.

I hurriedly walk back. I stop every now and then to record the site on video, but what am I recording? Mechanical documentation, or does the video reflect another mood that the site then was revealing to me?

Raindrops start to fall and glimmer on the yoni stones, which otherwise lie dry and dusty. The engraved pair of feet near them gets a ritual bath, like the traditional gesture of the weary traveller having her feet washed.

Today the stone feet are commonly read as belonging to a heroic warrior-king. They symbolize exile—the kind of exile that kings endured when they lost their kingdoms. The kings wandered into other lands, leaving their footprints as if to mark a new conquest. But shaktic texts point to other meanings, give another name: paduka, meaning 'feet' or 'wooden sandals'. It is another name for the goddess and the initiates who wander in her path, in her maya.

The rain intensifies, and the shrines' reflections shimmer in the dark, muddy waters. I take refuge in one shrine and contemplate the falling rain as the video records it into digital images. Another aesthetics of the site seems to slowly reveal itself. I experience a sense of wonder, another kind of calm, musing upon the rain bathing the shrines. This dissolves into apprehension as I return to another reality: it is getting dark, and I am worried about the video (getting wet) and the money that I am carrying in my various jacket pockets. These are the funds for my entire trip, a princessly sum that I am scared to leave behind in the hotel room but curiously not scared to carry around.

The rain slows to a drizzle and I head towards the jeep. I am always anxious about finding my way to the site, but never about returning. The outline of the factories is usually clearly visible, and indicates the way to the road and the spot where my jeep is parked.

I am usually so satiated by the experience of this site, with the sunset slowly disappearing into the horizon, that the return walk of a few kilometres is imbued with a meditative quality. Today there is no sunset, indeed hardly any light, and I do not want to end the day on a dissonant note. I walk faster. The rain intensifies. The thin drizzle changes to thick drops, which cascade down while the clouds thunder in orchestration. It is so dark that the factories are not visible. Panic clouds my navigation skills. I am lost. I walk almost an hour through the rain before I recognize a landmark: the metal road close to the highway, a detour of many kilometres. And I still have a four-kilometre walk to the jeep. I enter a factory and ask them if there is a car, bus or three-wheeler that can take me there. They look at me in perfect shock, as if to ask what I am doing here. I explain that I have just come from the Naresar temple site. They have never heard of it, and their expressions suggest that women should not be doing such crazy things—it detracts from their domestic role in life. Even these men would not venture out of their everyday by a kilometre if they could help it. My earlier panic starts to give way to anger.

Their world is that of industrialization. The cosmological lies adjacent, hidden yet accessible. My world is a strange inter-section of both. But the industrial world seems ignorant of these cosmologies, ignorant of their maya. Will this world take over the magic of the yogini sites by virtue of the illusion of its omnipotence?

An empty scooter-rickshaw shows up. I run towards it but see that a man has already occupied it. I shrug in disappoint-ment, but the scooter stops at my feet: the man has fetched it for me. The seat is almost as wet as I am, and the cold wind contributes to my state of chill. I guide the driver to the road where the jeep is parked. The sight of it sends a flood of warmth and relief through my core. I start to pay the driver, who stone-facedly asks five times the normal price. We fight. In fury, I fling a note and curse at him. Just as I start to drive, I notice that someone has taken the air out of one of the jeep's tyres. I left my electrical air-filling gadget in the hotel room. I fling another curse at the man or men who have deflated the tyre, and another still at myself for not foreseeing this possibility.

Shivering, I take the tyre off, but my hands are so cold that I have a hard time installing the replacement. A truck appears from a mud path. I stop it.

No problem, Madam, says the man who jumps out of the truck. With disdainful arrogance, he has the tyre back on with a couple of deft hand movements. I thank him and offer him some money. He refuses.

Life is ironic, after all.

Rest Stop: Orchha

On long journeys, planning routes is an art in itself. Distances, road quality and accommodation can make or break a trip. When I first started travelling, these elements were of no importance. I had limitless energy, excellent motor skills thanks to a background as a professional table-tennis athlete, the arrogance of youth and a hard-bull head. A few equally hard knocks on the head, a couple of accidents and a decade later, I have learnt that the body makes its own demands. After a hard day, a pleasant rest halt is highly recommended.

The next yogini stop is in Khajuraho, more than four hundred kilometres from Gwalior. The drive takes roughly twelve hours and is no difficult accomplishment, but I have learnt to insert Orchha as a rest stop. The 120-kilometre stretch from Gwalior to Orchha is hardly strenuous, in fact very pleasant; there is little industry and little traffic, so the Gypsy averages eighty to ninety k.p.h. without much vibration. The only crowded town to be passed is Jhansi. Halfway to Orchha lies a medieval palace city built by the Bundelkhand kingdom, which then had relative autonomy from the Mughals. There is also an old Devi temple, but I shudder to think what they've done to the site and cannot bring myself to visit it. It is a practising site with blaring loudspeakers.

The drive to Orchha is incident-free. The hotel I have

taken is again run by Madhya Pradesh Tourism, and consists of scattered cottages overlooking the river Betwa. The view has now been blocked by an illegal construction: another hotel. I am told that so much money has changed hands that no punitive action has been taken or will be taken, despite many official complaints.

When I first came here, Orchha was unknown to tourists. There was only one mid-range hotel, an old converted palace. The room in which I stayed had once been a servants' quarter. The building's many terraces overlooked other medieval palaces and had different views of the river. Never had I had such a feeling of being in a fairy-tale landscape—ruins everywhere, paintings still visible in some of the palaces, an old banyan tree growing through the ruins of an old stepwell, and the water of the river crystal-clear.

Today I sit for hours by the river, photographing the myriad reflections of light in the water. At sunset, Ushas glows over the town and flows through the water. This is the time of the day to listen to an evening raga. The palace courtyard, with its many terraces and splendid acoustics, would have been the optimal place for such a concert; indeed, it was perhaps through just such a combination of architecture and landscape that Hindustani ragas emerged in the form in which we know them now. People could sit on one of the terraces, each at a different height, and hear the soaring of notes, their modulations as they created their moods in harmony with the changing light, landscapes and seasons. Sheltered under a terrace, people could watch the pouring of the monsoon rain, could feel the heat of the earth erupting into an eros of wetness while the sounds of *Megh Malhar* crescendoed to the lightning and thunder.

The arts and intellect are governed by the goddess Sarasvati—she who has the beautiful ras. *Ras* can mean essence, juice, mood, emotion. Each art form had as its ideal the embodiment and unfolding of a certain ras. It was the occupation of the queens and the bais to create, enact, perform and manage these cultures. Each art form had its yogini; sixty-four forms for the sixty-four yoginis.

Women musicians are depicted in the palace murals and stone carvings, but it is the signatures of the men that are stamped today in the musical annals. The bai as a priestess of the arts, of the mood (ras) of Shringhar (eros), as the priestess of the goddess Sarasvati, is perceived today as a courtesan-prostitute. What histories have been swept away by this stroke of shifting meanings?

Today it is not the notes of the *Megh Malhar*, which are sung, or the sunset and dawn ragas. It is ear-splitting loud-speakers emitting Bollywood film music with modern Hindu lyrics. 'Religious pop', it's called.

A decade ago, 'Hindu' identity did not have to be violently attested, did not need sound and other forms of propaganda. Today Ram has become a mirror reflection of the Islamic Rahim, the goddesses crushed and domesticated. Yet it is said to be the Kali era, the time of the yoginis, the time of the great war.

The brahmins are evidently scared. The myth of the Kaliyug states that women will head their families again. The lower castes and the outcasts (mlechh) will govern society, and the existing caste system will disappear. All the tabooized sexualities will celebrate their pleasure rituals, and the population will decrease!

River Routes

The river Betwa is not well known, though it flows through Bhopal, the capital of Madhya Pradesh. As a child, I was familiar only with the Ganga of the northern plains. My earliest memories of this river date from when I was three. The river was inextricably bound to the rhythmic movement of a train, and I was overwhelmed equally by the huge bridges and the broad river that lay under them. Added to this was the pleasure of throwing coins in the river and making a wish. To a three-year-old the concept of a wish did not have much relevance, but I loved watching the falling of the coin in the waters, making a barely visible ripple and disappearing in its infinitude.

The Betwa is not so wide, but it has taken on a magical quality. Without realizing it I have followed its course to a place called Deogadh—the city of the gods. The road ends here; it is literally the back of beyond, a little village with a small guest house that is empty most of the year. This little stretch lies in Uttar Pradesh, though it is surrounded by Madhya Pradesh and referred to in the Sanskrit texts as *madhya desh*.

Opposite the guest house loom some temples, earlier than any I have seen in the vicinity of Gwalior. They are classified by local archaeologists as belonging to the Gupta period, the second to fifth centuries. Temple remains from this period are scarce and hardly documented; these are like precious jewels. But they are not my destination—I am looking for the yogini site at Dudhai. My journey will not be complete if I do not visit at least three yogini sites. I am not convinced about the accuracy of my reference book. Often when sites are difficult to access, scholars do not put in the energy to actually locate them, giving instead an approximate marking that often mixes up directions. To me, the journey to these sites is an essential part of such research.

The guest house is locked and appears empty. I look around trying to find someone who will serve us a cup of tea and might have heard of our destination. After a few minutes a young man named Malkhan emerges from one of the hitherto locked doors. He is happy to have visitors. When my companion says she loves the calm of the place, Malkhan, thrilled, gives us the best room in the house. I ask him about Dudhai.

A perplexed frown crowds his sensitive face. A few minutes later he says he knows of a chowkidar who may have worked at the site about five years ago. He disappears, and half an hour later he is back with the chowkidar, who does remember the site. It is close by—only about fifteen kilometres away, not even an hour's drive. I ask him if there is a metalled road all the way.

Thora jungle mein jana parega. We will have to go through the jungle.

Will the jeep go? I inquire.

Yes, definitely—no problem. Bas ek-do kilometre hi hai.

When did you last make the trip?

Kuch sal ho gaye. A few years ago.

How many years?

About five.

Gari gayi thi? Did the car make it?

Nahin, phas gayi thi—it got stuck. The minister was with us.

Did you reach?

No. The minister did not want to walk.

51

I try to interpret his answers. 'Fifteen kilometres' means at least thirty. One or two kilometres of unmetalled forest path could mean at least five. Thirty kilometres of bad road would take me at least an hour, and five kilometres of forest track could take thirty to forty-five minutes—and that's if the track is still jeepable. Then there would be at least a few kilometres of walking. I had already driven four hours that morning. I hesitate, but Malkhan is persistent. He is dying of boredom, his sensitivity and intelligence suffocated in this tiny village. He himself is eager to see more of the ancient civilizations that lie around him. My companion is excited by the possibility of a new adventure. Enthusiasm is infectious. The decision is made.

The road gets progressively worse as fifteen kilometres come and go. Another fifteen slowly disappear behind us. We turn off into the forest. After about two hundred metres, I start having nightmares that the jeep will get stuck, will turn over. This is no track; there are only stones. The jeep tilts at various angles.

A tree lies across the stones. I am determined not to drive any more but walk—yet my companions are adamant. They succeed in pushing the fallen tree to one side, and to my horror we continue. A few kilometres later, there is a sharp ascent. I have to make it, as I cannot turn the jeep around. The others get off and walk on in total confidence. I do make it, and to my astonishment we are at the ruins of an old colonial building. More than a hundred years ago, it was the bungalow and forest rest house of the white sahibs.

A little further on is an ancient bridge. The British evidently repaired it, but there is no river left. The chowkidar informs me that the river turned poisonous almost a hundred years ago, and the villagers fled to another terrain despite this being strictly forbidden under colonial law. Rerouting any river—indeed, any large-scale migration—was heavily punishable. People could have their hands and feet cut off. Mass movements could lead to impossible administrative problems, a collapse of Her Majesty's bureaucracy.

More than any historical analysis of colonialism, this fact of controlling the river waters, controlling village movement, was for me one of the most powerful insights into the centuries of imperial power. It is uncanny to park the jeep here and look through the crumbing walls—this was, after all, a prototype for the forest guest houses or travellers' bungalows littered all over India. They were the edifices, the fulcrums of the colonial bodies.

A temple looms over the other side of the bridge. But it is the abandoned village houses that throw me out of gear. An empty, desolate, dead village where the houses are made not from mud but from stones—stones left over from temple ruins.

I ask the chowkidar if he remembers where the yogini temple is.

Woh kya hota hai? What is that?

I change my strategy and ask, Koi gol mandir tha, khula, jismein murthiyan thi? Was there any round temple, open, with sculpture?

Han, aise kuch to tha laikin ab yar nahin. Mandir to das kilometre tak parte hain. There was something like that but I don't quite remember. The temples extend ten kilometres.

Every few hundred metres lie broken pieces of temple walls and sculptures. We find more temples representing a range of different divinities. Did they coexist, or did they replace each other? There are said to be countless billion divine possibilities;

53

the problem lay in finding one's *sv-isht* devi or devata, the desired divinity of the self. Did finding one's own divine constellation lead to the profound tolerance and acceptance of another's, unless it violated one's own? Did the other pole of monotheism represent not the dominance of a hierarchical, savage, absolute godhead but the respect in the subjective metaphysical search?

The yoginis are again elusive. My companion is tired and thirsty, and the sun is at its strongest. I cannot leave till I find the site. My bull-headed energy takes over. I spot some people from the nearest village working on one of the archaeological sites and ask them about the temple, describing it in detail. No, they have no idea. I reframe the questions.

Was there any kind of maidan, (ground) in shape?

There is a wrestling ground [akhada] nearby.

They point in the direction of the shrub jungle. It is difficult to find a path, but I persist; overgrown, unkempt bushes with needle-like branches get incessantly entangled in my clothes. But there is not a trace of any temple stone. Obstinately, I hang on to my intuition. After what seems like an eternity of walking, a clearing appears, surrounded by a broken wall.

I know I have found the temple, and sure enough, what to the villagers is a wrestling ground is a yogini temple, round and open to the sky, with small niches. The yoginis have gone to museum godowns, or have simply flown out of their stone form. It does not matter; the temple is there, and the centre is free.

The return to the guest house is uneventful. Malkhan asks if we can stop on the way to pick up groceries. The nearest village to the guest house is nine kilometres away; Malkhan must walk there for provisions, or wait for the occasional bus. There is no infrastructure: no telephone in the guest house, no gas for cooking, only a small heater that he procured with much difficulty. The UP Tourism brochure advertises this as a six-room guest house with the luxury of running hot water, but only two rooms are actually functioning. Everything has to be cooked on the small, one-coiled heater, including hot water for a bath. A power cut or the collapse of the coil means no food. Malkhan is one of those rare people who manages, against all odds, to keep his thoughtfulness alive. It was thanks to him that this place still existed, and was not a derelict like the colonial bungalow.

Why, I ask him, did UP Tourism build this guest house if they were so apathetic about running it?

It was the work of an IAS officer. The temples were in ruins. Kisi ko parvah nahin thi (No one cared). Sahib loved this place, and he wanted to create a rest house so others could observe its beauties. It is thanks to him that some of these temples are now looked after.

Malkhan speaks with a deep respect for this anonymous Indian officer. Despite its suffocating loneliness, he loves this place, too. He asks us if he can show us another special place at sunset.

After lunch my companion and I venture to the so-called Jain temples atop a small hill. What awaits us inside is unbelievable. The shrines for the Jain figurines have been turned into little cells, and the pillars have been walled and plastered over with more figurines. The result is unforgivable kitsch. Broken pieces of sculpture have been montaged together in the most absurd combinations. A broken female head rests on an elephant trunk, her hand attached to the trunk. She is painted pink and green.

We come back in a state of shock, not knowing whether to cry, laugh or scream in rage.

Malkhan is waiting for us, and expects our reaction. He tells us how the Jains took over the site a year ago. To whom do I complain, to whom do I protest? he asks sadly. Meri kaun sonega? Who will listen to me?

He suggests we take the jeep. I would much rather walk, but he says there's not enough time. We will miss the sunset. I trust him completely. We drive back to the hill but turn on to a small track at its base, and there is another Gupta temple. Just the sight of it is enough to exorcise the earlier horror. We leave the jeep and walk down some stairs leading to the river. The Betwa is luminescent in the Ushas light. As we descend the gorge almost to the foot of the riverbank, Malkhan takes us into a cave. It is finely sculpted with matrikas, almost two thousand years old.

Adya Shakti

The yogini temples are known to be difficult to access. Of those I have visited, each but one has been imbued with the pleasure of discovery after an arduous search. It is as if the search is looking for the needle in the haystack, its experience and discovery the threading of the needle. But there is one yogini site I visit repeatedly that I simply came to as if by invitation. It lies at a major tourist stop: Khajuraho.

Like Dudhai, Khajuraho is a temple city. Over thirty temples have been unearthed, and there are still some to be discovered. It is a World Heritage Site renowned for its sexual iconography, perceived as the *Kama Sutra* in stone. Agra is famous for the Taj Mahal, Banaras for its spiritual cemetery on the river Ganga; Khajuraho becomes the sexual climax of this jet-setting tourist triangle. During the season, plane- and busloads of tourists come daily to marvel at the carvings. Cafes abound, the local economies flourish and many villagers speak a khichdi of different languages. A smattering of European tongues interspersed with Japanese, Korean and now Hebrew comprises the linguistic and culinary platter.

A few decades ago, Khajuraho was just as difficult to access as Dudhai. A visionary IAS officer is said to have contributed to its development, restoration and subsequent fame by the initial act of getting an access road built. The path through the jungle was replaced by a metalled road, even better in quality then the highway to which it is linked. Later the airport was built.

My first entry to Khajuraho fifteen years ago was not through the quick air transfer but on the road in the avatar of a taxi driver. It was the result of a strange coincidence. I had been in Berlin, wanting to return to Delhi as soon as possible. I had a standby ticket, the lowest in the hierarchy of free tickets. I was told that the sector from Berlin to Frankfurt would be no issue, but there was a substantial risk of being stranded in Frankfurt. The counter in Frankfurt's airport was thronged with passengers. The suspense of waiting made knots of tension in my stomach. Slowly, passengers started to leave the counter and go towards their onward destination. An announcer started to read the names of the standby passengers, but my name was not among them. The last trickle of passengers was dissolving when finally my ears caught the familiar syllables of my name. A boarding card was pushed at me with a gesture to rush. I was through.

My relief slowly gave way to exhilaration as the air hostess passed me by. A look of recognition flashed mutually in our eyes: we had been friends at school, travelling companions in the same school bus. Almost fifteen years had passed since our last meeting. She excused herself and came back with a glass of champagne.

Subsequently, as we were chatting in the small kitchen space, a Dutch woman in her sixties joined us. She was travelling to India for the first time. I gave her my phone number and offered to help her arrange train tickets. In Delhi, just before she bought the tickets, she asked if I would instead be her taxi driver and companion. I had just bought my jeep and was looking for clients. I accepted immediately.

I must tell you something first before you finally decide, she said.

Confusion frowned across my face. She was my first client; I did not want to lose her.

I am Jewish, she said. I could not travel on my Israeli passport, as India does not recognize us. It has been my dream to come to India so I used my Dutch passport. I am sorry I did not tell you earlier.

Come home with me, then, I automatically replied. Why stay in a hotel?

When the Nazis had established themselves in Holland, Betteke had barely been twelve years old. Her mother had been deported, but she and her eldest sister succeeded in finding separate hiding places. Her middle sister had already migrated to Palestine. When the war was over, she had wished only to leave Holland, to leave the legacy of brutality and butchery as far behind as possible. Hers was a lost generation—lost in mourning, in rage, in despair, in relief, clueless about their destiny. She arrived in Palestine shoeless.

I ask hesitantly about her family.

We found each other soon, my sisters and my mother. Everyone else was murdered.

My grandfather was a doctor in the British army. He was stationed in Palestine during the war, and there he met some Jewish families from Central and Eastern Europe. He had been wined and dined and intellectually stimulated; I suspect he even fell in love. He did not talk much about his many travels, and never about the war, but he must have told me over a hundred times about the hospitality he had experienced in Palestine. Escaping the narrowness of his own Indian upbringing in Lahore, including the pressures of a child marriage, he had become in his own way an outsider. Neither a nationalist nor a colonialist, he had existed in the cracks, drifted from place to place, perhaps never even developed a need for home. Where was home for him? Not in his family; his mother had given him away to her mother-in-law, as his younger brother had been her favourite. Little is known about this brother except that he committed suicide.

The family secrets are deeply buried. What little I have been able to ascertain has come through the stray stories that occasionally fall my way. My grandfather never spoke of his parents, only of his grandparents. His sole source of love was his grandmother, who protected him from the eccentric tyranny of his grandfather. It must have been a curious threesome: the patriarch at the apex, the wife and grandson forming a curious alliance at the bottom of the triangle.

When he was fourteen, my grandfather's marriage was arranged without his knowledge. My grandmother was twelve. My grandfather only thought of flight—flight from this child bride, flight from his family, flight from the value system he found himself entrenched in. Resistance to his father took the form of his learning medicine, a firangi occupation, the fake science of the colonial invaders. He could have followed in his father's footsteps and became a forest officer. They were kings of their domain: they had their fiefdom, any woman they wanted, perhaps a grand bungalow and handsome salary. Instead my grandfather left the family, left the city of Lahore to study in Bombay.

I often wonder about their conflict. Was my grandfather illegitimate? Was that why he was given away? What kind of mother, especially in India, would give her son away? A complex jigsaw puzzle, most of whose pieces are safely locked up. Only odd bits of information spill out. Thus, one morning my grandmother casually told me not the secret of my grandfather's birth, but the drama of his father's death.

My grandfather was with his father in his forest fiefdom. His father got bitten by a snake, and none of his scientific knowledge could be put to use. He could only be a silent and knowing spectator to his father's death. Was that the ending of their unresolved conflict?

Disillusioned with Indian nationalism, deprived after Partition of his one homestead, my grandfather must have found in Tel Aviv and Jerusalem a kind of visionary home space—he was the valued guest. And now, through my encounter with Betteke, he could extend a return hospitality.

Six hundred kilometres and two weeks later, Betteke and I arrived in Khajuraho. We explored the area as best as we could. Temples everywhere, sculptures everywhere. Overwhelming. Unfamiliar. I knew the different revolutions in European art, the different epochs, the cultural nuances, but these forms of sculpture exploded the frontiers of my consciousness. How was I to contextualize them? What was I being initiated into?

After satiating ourselves with rows and rows of detailed sculpture, I found the path to the yogini temple. People looked at us, shrugged their shoulders and replied with a disgruntled wave of the hand: Kuch nahin hai. There is nothing. We persisted.

Across the fields, behind the main temple complex, stands a rectangular temple on a mound. It is open to the skies, with all the niches in its inner walls empty. The central space is free, and as the sun set on that first visit I intuitively grasped that the temple had been built on the West–East axis: a cosmic stage on which the sun could descend and the moon rise amidst a liminal carpet of stars.

The yogini temple is the oldest temple in Khajuraho. It is the temple that first 'initiated' me, inspiring me to return again and again.

Thirteen times have I now been to Khajuraho, and each time I must start my journey in this temple, listening to the symphony of the sunset light before I begin any other exploration. It was there at the beginning, the punar. It was the source of every temple subsequently built in Khajuraho.

Punar is a Sanskrit word that expresses a primal beginning.

61

It also means a return to this beginning; the movement of return is likened to an eternal homecoming. Is this temple a home, its minimality a source to which I must return in order to carry on as an eternal wanderer, a paduka?

And what does its architecture configure? A rectangular space open on each end, the back opening miniscule and the front opening majuscule. The back portal is like the eye of the needle, but it is adjacent to the largest niche. Geometrically and mathematically, it seems to convey the confluence of the other niches. Philosophically, the passage between the portals appears to be a path to the free centre, to the primal formless energy around which emerges the sum of all the yoginis, the sum of the infinite potential.

Infinity is formless—beyond numbers, beyond boundaries —yet it is the possibility of all forms, the sum of different individuated details. Each detail is unique, yet part of an underlying cosmological unity. A unity that is not a homogenized 'one' but a 'zero', infinitely intricate.

Is the form of the temple earlier than that of the sculptures? Were the sculptures a later addition, another kind of memory as the living traditions died? Did women inhabit the site as living yoginis, meditate in the niches, build these mounds and these temples? Archaeologists and historians are puzzled as to who built these sites; no kingly reference is available. To acknowledge authorship by women, by yoginis themselves, would be to acknowledge and collapse their own mental prisons and lakshman-rekhas.

Yet there is an abundance of information in sculpture, architecture and even inscription—enough to begin decoding these mysteries.

Yoginis and Bhairavs

The next station of this curvaceous journey takes me to Orissa. My research indicates two yogini temples there. One is in a village called Hirapur, near Bhuvaneshwar, and the other is in Ranipur Jharial, in western Orissa not far from the Madhya Pradesh border.

The express train from Delhi to Bhuvaneshwar covers more than 1,700 kilometres, yet distance is no measure of time. It takes twenty-four hours, but a smaller town closer to Delhi but not on the express-train network can easily take more than twice that time. Express trains have priority status; passenger trains must wait for them. The waiting time on passenger trains far surpasses the moving time. Just when one thinks that the train is picking up speed, and one is allowing one's thoughts to meander along with the fleeting landscape, the train screeches to a halt. It sits. People curse and sigh in exasperation, resignation. A man gives a long tirade: how long will the train stop this time? The train arrived eleven hours late, and now it waits. Forty-five kilometres should take one hour, but how long will the train wait now? Eleven hours?

Train journeys are a cultural experience, particularly of philosophies of time. I used to be amazed that in Switzerland, one could catch a connecting train with only five minutes of waiting time. Once I got used to this clockwork precision, a delay of five minutes would render me angry and impatient as a delay of five hours in India would not do.

One time the train in Geneva was twelve minutes late. An announcement was made: The train is running twelve minutes late, but this is not our fault. It has been delayed in Italy.

Long Indian train journeys: slow time, stretchable time, monotonous time, meditative time, waiting time, and above all *timepass*. The vendors come, often young boys screeching in castrato voices: 'Timepass, timepass! One rupee, one rupee!' They are selling a mixture of nuts in small cones of newspaper.

Timepass, like bypass, is a fundamentally Indian concept. Life is time in suspension. Life is a process of waiting, observation, ennui—time is simply to be *passed*. The train, the railway platform becomes its stage. People come, people go, luggage is shoved in wherever there is an opening. Coolies push their way in, blocking seats. Fights occur. There is a constant cacophony of voices as goodbyes are said, reunions take place and something or the other is transacted. Peddlers are everywhere, stands on wheels making their rounds of the train's windows. Beggars of all sizes and shapes, travelling musicians, fakirs, train-side palmists and astrologers are only some of the kaleidoscopic images of station platforms. The train comes to a standstill but the market continues. Life is one big tamasha, one big bazaar.

Kali sits in a marketplace, holding an array of colourful kites in her many hands. They fly through the congested lanes, their colours matching the bustle of life. Every now and then, a few fly away. She laughs—a full, raucous laughter.

Finding the village of Hirapur is not easy. The bus leaves us at the river, and we walk our way about the many fields, searching for more than two hours. The villagers, apparently scared of the temple, are hesitant to tell us the way. When we finally find the temple, the sun is setting and we cannot see the sculptures clearly.

But the temple calls me back. A few months later a friend invites me to Bhuvaneshwar and lends me his motorcycle to visit the archaeological sites. He introduces me to his friend B, a man in his sixties. B's face has an ageless intensity and a rare vitality, and radiates warmth and a sharp intelligence. He was a pilot in the air force, but was almost court-martialled due to a combination of his asthma and his homosexuality. He lives as a recluse in a huge bungalow, in which he has a studio and a kiln for pottery. Like my grandfather, he was unable to resist an arranged marriage, and his homosexuality and artistic disposition led to constant friction within the family. Despised for not living unto the material family scales he is seen as a social outcast, an eccentric who lived life on his own terms in accordance with his philosophies, aesthetics and erotic sensibility. His vision is to regenerate artisanal traditions, particularly those lost in the amnesia of time—to remake three-thousand-year-old terracottas as finer renewals, in which the 'copy' goes further than the 'original'.

What is the original? What is a copy? A dualism that plagues the European artistic mind.

An artist dies in poverty; later the work is sold for millions. But a brilliant copy has no artistic significance, only monetary value if it can pass for an original. How absurd! In India, we seek a continuum. We seek out the motif, we study the process by which it was created, we try to understand the pulse of the process, its context, and in remaking it we breath new life into it, renewing its memories and creating our own traditions and continuums.

Our philosophies meet as our words concur. B. explains to me the terracotta process while I lay out the etymological roots of *rit*, of this philosophy and its connections with my own erotic continuum.

rit	=	the pulse of life, its throb
M + rit	=	death (*m* indicates a reversal)
A + mrit	=	eternal, elixir (*a* indicates negation)
S + mrit(i)	=	memory (*s* indicates preservation, keeping alive)

Death is not an end but a form of amnesia. To remember is to regenerate life and initiate a new beginning, a new cycle. Every end lies between two beginnings. It is like the older homoerotic philosophies of the twin, the jami. The eros between the twins is a form of attraction to both what is similar and that which is different. The ecstasy of their meeting generates a fusional moment wherein the two become one, yet do not lose their specificities. They are one and two at the same time, opening up a third space.

A + jami—that which is not jami, i.e., heterosexual—is predicated on a binary opposition between two genders. Their union is a homogeneous merger, a reduction of differences into a monolithic universal.

B showed me the new collections of graphics he has painted, a series of triangles. The concordance is uncanny.

Later, as we discuss the sites' locations, their situationality in relation to the river, I mention my impending visit to the yogini temple. You should take the direct route over the small bridge, he tells me. That is the most erotic temple I know in all of India. It is the only temple built on the other side of the river.

I take the direct route. The narrow bridge takes a motorcycle but cannot take any larger form of transport. By the time I arrive, it is midday. It is the beginning of summer and sweltering-hot. The temple is tiny, the smallest temple I have experienced. Opposite the temple entrance is a constructed mound, a raised platform. Two arches frame the temple's free central space. Undeterred, the local brahmin priest has created his own centre: the yogini opposite the entrance, in a niche in the peripheral wall. She has been covered with a shiny red cloth. I take it off to find a deliberately mutilated figure—only the torso is left. The other sculptures too have been badly smashed. They were all built from a metallic black stone, not the customary sandstone.

To enter the temple I have to bend my head, so tiny is the entrance. To photograph the yoginis, I have to sit on the ground. The temple seems to have been built on a micro scale—an aesthetics of concealment. It is strikingly different from the temples of Bhuveneshwar.

The temple's other unusual aspect is that there were sculptures on its outside wall. In addition, there are four pillars within the central space, forming a pair of arches. The space between them is free, but there are carvings on all the pillars. They create a square, its corners marked by pillars sculpted with two pairs of male figures and two pairs of yoginis.

```
        M M
    F       M
    F       M
        F F
```

The male figures in this tradition are known as bhairavs. Their identity stems from their having given up their masculine ego (viry), and thereby establishing another relationship to the

67

feminine within and without. The bhairavs here have erect penises, but these point upwards—the urdhva position, from which sexual energy flows upwards and is not penetrative. The goal is to attain a still consciousness, represented by a small head. Its name: Sada Shiv. The eternal Shiv.

Sada Shiv is one side of the myth of Sati and its dramaturgy.

The prelude starts with Daksh, the bramanical father of Sati, preparing a huge sacrifice. The lower-caste tamasic son-in-law Shankar is not invited, nor is his daughter Sati. She is now the appendage to another man's caste. However, Sati insists on going despite Shankar's insistence to the contrary.

Sati: I will go and you will give me your permission. And if they, the fools in front of me, abuse you, I will destroy the sacrifice—no doubt.

Shankar: You will go to hear them abuse me. Why do you wish to go for that?

Sati: I am not going to hear the abuse, but because of the festival. You are not the picture of irreverence. Nobody is; rather, the gathering is for the respect of Ahuti. Therefore, I will go with or without your permission. If the sacrifice is not sacred, I will destroy it and make it festive.

Shankar: Mahadevi, when you will not listen to me, you commit sin. I know you of many words, the daughter of Daksh, that you will act according to your wish. Then why do you want my permission?

Narrator: Thus hardly had the great god spoken whereupon Sati, in her contemplation, became enraged in a moment and replied:

Sati: You requested me in the role of a wife, but now that you have insulted me, see me as I am. Shambhu, I will disclose to you my forms of anger.

Narrator: Eyes (of Sati) blazing with the heat of darkness

Eyes (of Shankar) becoming closed

The fierce middle teeth in the powerful face, laughing raucously

While the great god is entranced with fear

Abandoning her white form and her old state, Sati becomes without clothes, her hair freed, red-tongued, four-handed, adorned with a garland of skulls, a half moon on her forehead, shining with glowing heat.

Shankar, in fear upon seeing this form, tries to run away but is encompassed from all ten directions by Sati's manifestations of the beyond, the peripheries—*para*. When Sati discloses her Kali forms to Shankar, she tells him to find his inner form: that of the Sada Shiv.

Later, when Shankar comes looking for her and sees only her shadow body, in a rage he beheads the father, Daksh. Then a reconciliation occurs. Daksh is given a goat's head, and in return Shankar receives a portion of the sacrifice. The sacrifice is only partially destroyed, and once the dark male side is integrated, the sacrifice is allowed to continue. But there is a cosmic shift. Daksh, instead of being the patriarchal brahmin father, becomes a devotee of Sada Shiv. The motif of the severed head and its subsequent replacement by the head of a goat—the animal often used for the sacrifice—is a homoerotic rite of transfer between the two male sublimated poles of the satvik and tamasic. There is no need for female objectification as mediation.

But the story has yet another level. Sati returns home.

Thus the goddess of the south, with free-flowing hair, beautiful, descends from her carriage, and both mother and daughter fuse in an embrace again and again—part of the sanskritic text attributed to an absent narrative voice.

> *Daksh* (on seeing Sati in her transformed, liberated form): Who are you? Whose daughter are you? (You) woman, gone asunder, back off from here.
>
> *Sati*: Father, how is it that you do not recognize your Sati? You are my father and I am your daughter. I greet you.
>
> *Daksh*: Why have you become of the dark genre, like your mother? Why are you dressed in such a loose way at my gathering? Why is your hair free, and why are your eyes so fearful? What was the point of procuring a husband to see you so transformed? You are not invited to my sacrifice and my punar. In your fearful form, you are equivalent to the self-sexual.

At these words, another dramatic transformation takes place: Once more Sati takes on a shadow form. The verdict is spelled out:

> 'The sacrifice will be destroyed and the father killed.'
> Thus spoke Mahakali, Shadow-kali and Hasnamukhi.

After the verdict Sati makes her exit, leaving her shadow form behind. To the sheer stupefaction of the entire male pantheon, the abandoned body does not burn; rather, the sacrificial fire is extinguished.

Mahamaya and her band of yoginis manifest themselves

The autumnal full moon creates twelve yearly cycles of rain

The deluge occurs to all those present/invited at the Daksh's sacrifice

A rain of flowers showers down and the sacrificial site is transformed into a shamshan ghat, with the wolves and jackals of Kali feasting on the remnants of those present.

—*Mahabhagvat Puran*

The Sati myth, like this temple across the river from Bhuvaneshwar, is part of a continuum in which plural sexual possibilities can coexist. But this is not how the story is told. The priest eloquently tells me there was once a central figure, a handsome, virile Shiv; unfortunately, someone stole it. The yoginis are only his servants.

The story is the same in Orissa's other yogini temple, in Ranipur Jharial: A bhairav figure has been cemented to one of the inner walls. I mention this to the ex-prince who discovered the temple. He had no interest in archaeology and led a typical life of leisure, until one day he had an accident and went into coma for several days. No one knew whether he would wake from it or sink into a more permanent sleep. When he woke, he felt compelled to go out and unearth the archaeological memories around him. Some time later, he discovered the presence of this yogini temple.

Ah, the bhairav, he said. It comes from one of the neighbouring sites. The local villagers found it and put it in the centre so they could celebrate their rituals.

A year later, I return to both these temples. The yoginis in Hirapur are again covered with oil, the finesse of their detail covered up. A large American group, part of some modern Hindu sect, is on a spiritual yatra, chanting *Shiva—Shiva—Ram—Ram* as loudly as they can.

B died a month after our meeting. He had an asthma attack and was gone in a flash. His family had the last word, took their final revenge: They destroyed every last one of his artworks.

But I retain their memory.

Contradictory Nirvanas

The fourth yogini temple on this route, on this curve is in a small village called Bhedhaghat, roughly halfway between Khajuraho and Ranipur Jharial. I have been dreading the road to Bhedhaghat—approximately half of the three hundred kilometres from Khajuraho are in virtual disintegration. They kill my nerves, my back; it is shock treatment for the body and the jeep.

They are actually three routes to Bhedhaghat. I enquire at the local taxi stand about their respective states of being. The driver gives me a look of emphatic sympathy and says, Sab bekar hain. They are all useless. It is always a case of choosing the lesser evil.

I choose the road that goes through Panna National Park. The forest is old, and its interiors hide many old ruined temples. Today they are part of an offbeat tour offered by the Swiss cafe in Khajuraho, which leads jeep trips to the outlying areas, the waterfalls, the wildlife forests and the favourite local novelty—a treetop cafe and house run by another Swiss expatriate.

The Swiss cafe, one of the oldest restaurants in Khajuraho, is managed by an eminently unmarried French-Swiss woman. In all my travelling in India, I have never seen another cafe run by a lone woman. Now in her seventies, she came over thirty years ago from Geneva. Of her two sisters, only one remained in Geneva, and that sister has been her main link with Switzerland. Her other sister also lives in India, running a cafe in another remote area. They have created their Europe here.

The Khajuraho cafe offers plum-jam pancakes. She buys the fresh, cheap plums in huge quantities from the Himalayas, to which she retreats during the heat of summer, and sells them back to tourists as a delicacy. The cafe also has a bookshop, which must have been one of the first bookshops in Khajuraho. For international tourists, there are books on travel and Indian art. For arranged-marriage Indian honeymooners, there is *Playboy*.

I wonder what led her to exchange the Alps for summer in the Himalayas, the city of Geneva for the village of Khajuraho. This time she does not seem her usual active, energetic self but appears to be lost in her own memoric reveries. Is it the process of ageing, or the recent death of her countryman, owner of the treehouse?

Perhaps she, too, will die in India rather than Europe. It is a strange, beautiful knowledge, that of being able to choose the place of one's death.

Exhausted, I start for Bhedhaghat. The road is nightmarish. Just when it starts to improve, the unmarked speed breakers begin. Speed breakers are not allowed on National Highways, but each village has at least three, always unmarked. There is

73

a regular war of attrition between truckers and villagers, as children, adults and animals are regularly run over. The National Highway should ideally not go through any village, but the road brings 'progress'—trade and access to industrial development. Thus the villages grow on highway roadsides while the smog of the brick factories drastically pollutes the otherwise bare environs. Inhumane are the working conditions.

Finally I come to Jabalpur, fourteen kilometres from Bhedhaghat. Endless blowing of horns, open sewage pipes, collapsing roads, dense, chaotic traffic—all the typical horrors of organic, unplanned, mismanaged urbanization. It takes over an hour to drive through this mess.

What a contrast Bhedhaghat is—a beautiful scenic site, narrow marble gorges through which the river Narmada flows. It is the only river in India that flows from east to west. At the small guest house on the hill overlooking the river, there is a serene garden where one can relax to the tranquillity of the setting sun above the still waters while the marble gorges reflect its various sheens.

But this time the serenity is broken. Someone has just had a child, and the loudspeakers blare Indian disco and film music from a small hut.

My Nirvana is shattered.

Nirvana

Years ago, I was hitching in Europe. A young Canadian hitchhiker struck up a conversation—he was thrilled that I was Indian. He told me he had been looking for Nirvana, and had heard that he should be able to find it in India. Was this true?

His words repulsed me. They reinforced the disdain I had for both the word *Nirvana* and the inanity of the supposedly spiritual search of naive Westerners. I saw their quest as, at best, part of an absurd, exotic, veiled projection of 'India'. Needless to say, India has long offered an unsurpassed spiritual industry, with gurus, Sai Babas, Ammas, Matajis, ashrams and millions of deities on display and for sale.

For a long time, the concept of Nirvana was firmly entrenched in these projected havens. But one day I discovered a completely different meaning. I was travelling in the women's compartment of a Bombay local train. A hijra appeared in the compartment, and at once the atmosphere changed. Looks of disgust and embarrassment mingled with sounds of protest. Oblivious to the women, the hijra shrugged her shoulders, clapped her familiar clap and started money. She came to me with a loud clap.

Paisa do, give me money, she said. I shook my head in refusal.

Why? she demanded.

Main bhi to tumhare jaisi hoon, I replied. I am like you.

She gave me a broad smile, put her arms around me and said, winking, Main kaam khatam karke aati hoon. I'll finish my work and come back.

On her return, she asked me if I had experienced Nirvana. I immediately followed her meaning and nodded my head.

Nirvanas are subjective, as are the utopias we seek. They correspond to our desired cosmologies, a concept now so alien. Monotheism is a given, a curse that pervades globalization. Hinduism is its new belligerent creation. How can one be born with a religion? Is not the sacred a search for one's own path among the billions of choices? Are not the sacred and the profane indelibly linked?

I am sitting in a small Tibetan cafe in the Himalayan mountains. Twelve people sit around a small narrow table. A chelum is passed around. There are three Indians and nine Europeans. A scruffy young Englishman starts a loud tirade:

Dirty fucking people, a land of thieves, no bloody culture. We gave it all to them

Something explodes in me. I take on the Kali avatar. He is stuttering by the time I am finished. Later in the day, one of the Indian men comes up to me. He is a sadhu, a holy man, an expert in yoga. He offers me tea.

Between sips, he confesses: Main to goonda hoon. I am just a con man. They come to me wanting spiritual knowledge. I have sex with the firangi women, foreigners. They send me tickets to visit them, but what will I do in their country? Here, at least I know my way around. I sell the tickets and can live here for a long time. I used to deal in ganja, but the police have become more brutal. They want more of a cut. And the sarkar wants to sell their sharab (alcohol)—it's a big profit for them. Hamara zamana nahin raha. This is no longer our world.

A little while later, one of the other Indian men comes up to me. He is an avid skier; skiing is his way of communicating with the mountains. Every day he gets up at 4.30 to take the first bus to the village of Madhi, at more than four thousand metres. He then walks up another ten kilometres, and only then is he able to ski. I ask him how he can afford to buy skis. He used to hire an old pair, but some time ago a European gave him this pair. His Nirvanic dream is to ski in the Alps.

The next morning I go to Bhedaghat's yogini temple. It is

situated on a small hill. There are steps to be ascended. The temple is round. The archaeologists have not taken the yoginis to museums; they are in their niches. They appear splendid, despite the habitual traces of violent disfigurement.

The centre, however, has been occupied. A newer temple was built some centuries later, conventionally defined. Parvati sits on Shiv's lap. The temple guardian identifies himself with the newer temple. The yoginis are to be feared, he says. Only if one can save oneself from their maya can one enter the temple in the centre.

The newer temple has a royal edict indicating who built it and when. There is no such edict for the yogini temple, yet each yogini has her signature, her name inscribed beneath her sculptural form. The script is older than the royal edict.

Who were the yoginis? The question emerges once more. Were they women who lived in these sites, the sculptures merely their divine self-portraits? What was the socio-cosmological nexus? A queen's palace is said to have been linked to the temple and to the river, which loops around the temple, by underground passages.

What is the symbolic importance of the mound, from every side of which the river can be seen? Once again the temple seems to have been open on two sides. The doorway that descends to the river is now closed off, as is the underground pathway on the other side. Was this to block the spatial flows and transform the original network of the river and the hill?

As an open space, the temple acted as a sundial. It was as if the sun and the yoginis were engaged in a play of light and shadow. At different times of day, different yoginis were lit up while others cooled themselves in the shadows. But the newer temple has changed that: It blocks the sunlight. Some yoginis are now in permanent obscurity.

After visiting the temple, I descend to the river and walk along to the waterfall. I see a line of shops selling marble figurines. Lingams abound, but the yoginis are conspicuously absent. Further away sit a row of beggars making pleas for money in the most pitiful of tones. One beggar seems oblivious to the others' voices—he is blind, and his concentration is focussed on his musical instrument. He plays his drum with a pair of carved twigs and sings his song: the thousand names of the Devi. He is not from the area, I am told. He is from the eastern part of the country, and wandered over a thousand kilometres to come here.

It is the Nirvanic moment, the climax of my yogini journey.

PART II

Descent into the Abyss: Bodenlosigkeit

My journeys continue, as does the trauma of movement, broken sleep, anguish-ridden nights, feverish dreams longing for a warm, unchanging bosom—an intuition of the impending clash inherent in the metaphor of driving—the intersection of many worlds—the animal and the human in this instant. The nilgai (blue bull) blindly charging across the car at its natural speed—equivalent to the car. I see it in time, but only to cut the impending impact; the car starts to topple. The abyss stares in my face. One momentary lapse and the game of life is over.

I walk slowly towards the abyss, each step measured and serene. I walk towards my destiny, my dastaan—I drive into it. I walk to its edge—gradually I descend over its threshold as the sense of stillness and calm engulfs me. The bottomless abyss receives me in its sinking endless bosom. It is as though it has been awaiting me. The roses in its garden bloom. One rose particularly strikes me. I know it from my childhood gulistan. Its petals brush my lips—flaming colours—red and yellow. Its name—the 'Kiss of Fire'.

in quest of a beauty
a beauty of the bottomless pit
in its myriadic forms
anguish
pain
yearning for a fragility lost
a fragility of fullness
the innocent beauty
of intense happiness
m'illumine l'immensità d'amore

Fleeting landscapes transform constantly as the jeep measuredly clocks up kilometres on its gauge. The season gradually shifts as the hours pass by: The sun becomes stronger. Winter is over, as the forests of central India change into dense cultivated cotton fields that mark the advent of the southern landscapes. The Deccan plateau has started. A sense of exhilaration overcomes me, a new phase of the journey has begun and with it a wonder of the unknown.

Images in motion—landscapes in motion—seasons in motion—a film reel unfolding to jeep time, dreamlike and reflective yet demanding the utmost concentration. Long-distance driving is like long-distance running—a test of endurance—a tempo to be precisely maintained like a tabla tal, tiredness to be kept at bay, moving over its threshold into another mental horizon. Is this the liminality that this pilgrimage demands—the *jouissance* of the moment beyond exhaustion? Its meditativeness?

The meditation continues—a meditation on time—its elemental flow—the quality of flowing water. Ungraspable in its timeless quality. My reverie continues as the rivers come and go. It is water—water that marks the signature of civilizations, rivers their weaving threads.

I feel I have grown up imbued with this meditative quality, the image of sitting besides a river and gazing into its reflections and beyond it as if its waters enshroud a secret—an indecipherable mystery—the riddle of the sphinx that has no answers—it simply exists.

The dry face of a river bed stares out at me. A heap of sewage garbage, colourful in its range of plastic bags, jumps in my face. It is the mirror of a certain modernity—mire. The image repeats itself. The mire is constant, but not the water.

Water must be better harnessed, whether for agriculture or for industry. The mathematics of more yield. The logic of progress.

Dry rivers are not a recent happening. Many rivers have expressed the changing curves of seasons, of the cyclic intensity in their ebbs and rises—the extreme heat and dusty aridness of the excruciating summer heat, the erotic release and sensuousness outpouring of the monsoon—the steady decline through the winter for the cycle to recommence again from zero. A threefold cycle, a threefold state expressive of the symbolic mythology of the opening and closing of the Devi's eye and the transitory movement between these two moments: the tri-ambika.

am	=	blood
amba	=	mother, river
ambak	=	eye
tri-ambak	=	three eyes, the yoni

The king, Shantanu, falls in love with Ganga as she rows him over the waters. He proposes marriage to her even though she is at the lowest rung of his caste hierarchy. But from her perspective, she is divine whereas he is a mere mortal. She outlines a contract: He must never question her actions. A son is born, and is promptly submerged back in her waters. The following year another son is born, and again is returned to the waters. Seven times in succession this occurs. The king, desperate for a male heir, insists on retaining the eighth son. Ganga leaves. The contract is over; the eighth son may live but will not continue the royal genealogy. He must remain unmarried, must not procreate. He must die only by the divine feminine: that which is neither 'feminine' nor 'masculine'.

The eighth son, called Bhishm, is a fierce warrior, and because he is outside the domestic family economy, he can devote himself totally to martial pursuits. In order to get his two step-brothers married, he kidnaps three sisters named Amba, Ambalika and Ambika. Two of the sisters have no problem—we are told—marrying the two brothers. However, Amba has a fiancée whom she has chosen herself. Outraged, she demands to go back to him, but he refuses to take her back as she is now impure, having resided in another man's house. She vows to take revenge on Bhishm. She asks all the male warriors to uphold her dignity, her female dharma—to avenge her—but they are all fearful of Bhishm. Eventually she takes to asceticism and becomes half river, half woman. As a river form, she only has water one third of the time. She is said to have dusht tirth (difficult, dangerous shores).

Meanwhile, in another royal family, a certain queen has only daughters—no less than seven. The king tells her that if

84

she does not produce a son she will be thrown out. The eighth child is born: Amba. The queen does not divulge this to her husband, and Amba is brought up a boy. She is eventually married to a princess, whereupon her biological identity emerges. A solution is conveniently found—the feminine gender is coveted by the forest-dwellers, the yakshs. He/they willingly trades his gender-sex, and Amba gets a new name: Shikhandani (peacock, plume).

The peacock motif can be traced back to Harappan grave pottery. Peacocks were carrion-eaters and also the vehicle of Sarasvati, the goddess of music, memory and cognition. In the pre-Vedic epoch, Sarasvati was the great river around which the different civilizations emerged.

Shikhandani fires an arrow. Bhishm is killed. The resolution of the eight takes place. The fire of the dry river floods all boundaries.

> Darkness there was, the foremost dark dwelling, undifferentiated, all water, enclosed by the void, that magnificent One, that which by heat came into being.
>
> —*Rig Ved*

Holy Waters

The Ganga is seen today as the grandest, most majestic of Indian rivers. Banaras, or Van-ras (Essence of the Forest), is one of its foremost spiritual destinations—the place where the river receives back the dead. A journey of tourist pilgrimage—its attraction the burning of dead bodies, corpses burning from morning to night all throughout the seasons. A ritual cleansing, but a cleansing of what?

I have an American client who feels the ardent need to see this city. I warn her that the monsoon has been heavy, and the city on the ghats is a mass of squalor—an immense network of small galis that serve as toilet grounds for animals and humans alike. She hires me as her navigator to buffer her from this excessive terror of excrement. I escort her morning, evening and night, negotiating with the boatmen to take us on long rides on the holy Ganga. I stare out at its expanse, at its changing lights, at the hordes of people plunging themselves in its waters with their matkas and soaps, collective ritual bathing—women in wet saris sticking to their skins, men in loincloths, sadhus in orange garb, casually smoking their chelums . . . business is in full flow. The banks are always busy with the turmoil of people, with flourishing businesses—children selling lamps and flowers to float on the holy waters, peddlers peddling their wares, beggars begging for alms, lepers sitting in a row on their own designated bank. Each ghat has its demarcation; there is no empty space on this river. Cheap guest houses abound, catering mainly to Indian pilgrims and low-budget tourists. The high-end hotels are far from the maddening crowds. An air-conditioned bus brings their groups to a certain point from which cycle-rickshaws pedal them to the boats and the silk shops. Everything is organized—everything has its complex networks—everything in what seems to be an endless chaos has actually an amazing intricacy of connections.

Only silence is elusive, as is a meditative calm. There is one exception: I look in amazement at the lone woman in orange, powerfully serene in her dhyan.

My client wants to go into the living temple. I wait at the threshold. It is against my faith to enter these enclosures, which are, after all, a complete caricature of my own cosmologies. Her first experience is one of horror. The floors are filthy, wet with a mixture of mud, oil, milk and stagnant water. I continue to marvel at the logic of taking one's shoes off so as not to desecrate the temple floor. The brahmins have, after all, as much a foot fetish as my client does. She later confesses to me that she disinfected her feet, but this does not deter her from visiting another temple. Again I wait at the doorstep with the camera equipment, as photography is not allowed and this gives me another excuse not to go inside. Over an hour passes before she re-emerges. She could not find her way out.

There is only one gateway to enter and to exit.

I find a young boatman to take us across the river to watch the sunset. The boatman chats merrily away with my client. This is, after all, the only possibility of contact he has with the other gender, and she seems flattered by his attention. He avoids me, thinking I am her boyfriend. I can finally be alone. For the first time I experience a sense of stillness—there are only birds on this shore. The vultures and eagles sit patiently, awaiting their daily carcasses. The ghats are just faintly visible in the dusk light.

Gradually the night descends, but my client does not want to return. She wants to complete her spiritual journey with a visit to the burning ghats. There is an elaborate economic hierarchy in this practice. The woods used for the pyre vary in price, and likewise the clothes and the oils used to dress up the body all indicate the family's social situation. Ceremonies of this nature, be they marriages or deaths, are a show of social status. For poorer people there is an electric crematorium.

The actual death rites are done by the lower castes, minus

the women, of course. The transaction is between men. Men from a lower caste prepare the pyre and the corpse, and the oldest male heir or relative ignites the body. We make our way up to the ghat, having to push our way through the crowds. There is barely elbow room; I carve out a small path. Smoke is everywhere. We are the only women. The young man preparing the pyre explains various details of the ceremony, including who may and may not be cremated. There are few taboos here; only children below a certain age and women who die during pregnancy may not be cremated. I forget to ask him about unmarried women and barren women.

> There is once the dusht kanya of a brahmin sage. He dies, but she still refuses to get married. She retreats into the forest and performs a great tapasya. The sages get nervous. A message is sent to her: Unless she gets married, the gates of their heavens will not receive her. She is old and wrinkled by then. A brahmin boy marries her for one night, on the condition that she give him half the good karma she has accumulated. The dowry is agreed upon. On the appointed night she transforms herself into a radiant woman, and the brahmin wants her to stay on. The moment dawn sets in, she leaves.
>
> —*Mahabharat*

It is a family tradition, he tells me. He does not remember how far back the lineage of this profession goes; many genealogies. The smoke is suffocating. He is suffocated by this legacy, too.

I would have liked to have studied, he says, but my family had little money. And who would do this work otherwise?

I catch the feeling of pride—it is a chosen profession, it has its uniqueness—one that leaves no choice. A strange marriage between the two castes who stand at the extremes of the social hierarchy—its fulcrum, its interdependence.

It is a world alien and yet so known to me. I have never been present at any of my family's marriage or death ceremonies. The person who was my father created his own continuum with his own tradition: His liver slowly destroyed by an excess of whisky, he simply refused to go into the hospital. He lived in a small hut amidst the ruins of his former gulistan, his mortgaged factory. He was never able to sell it, never able to reopen it. Once a rich prospective buyer came, but all he got from my father was literally the boot. He was kicked out for having no vision, only commerce.

He chose the moment of his death, or perhaps he only knew of it. One Thursday morning he cancelled his one remaining middle-class habit—the daily newspaper. Sunday he was peacefully serene. Early Monday morning he was found dead, lying nude on the floor. An old Sindhi tradition, to go as one comes, with nothing—nude. It is a mark of consideration to the living that no one undress the body.

The smoke is overwhelming, but my client seems obsessed by the sight of half-burnt bodies slowly receding into the nothingness of ashes. It is a sweltering night, and sweat drenches me. Finally she is ready to leave. We make our descent to the boat. As the boat pulls away, she sneaks some video of the burning pyres. Photography is expressly forbidden, but like many taboos, this one is constantly broken.

Suddenly my client bursts out: I'm dying, I'm dying! I can't breathe!

Should I throw her into the river? I wonder. I proceed to calm her, and somehow drag her to the shore.

A Coca-Cola, get me a Coke, she says in her shrill, piercing voice.

There is a Coke stand on the shore. I come back with the much-needed elixir. She gulps down a couple of tablets.

They are only sedatives. She responds to my expression and continues to video the lights on the waters.

The experience of the earlier tranquillity has left me. Only the feeling of absolute decay.

Island

jambu = ja + ambu (rising, being born from the waters)

My first archaeological destination in the south is the site of Nagarjunakond, on the banks of what was the Krishna river. The banks have disappeared, and so has the original temple city—submerged by that 'progressive' vision of the 1950s, a mega-dam. An island has been created. The barque that ferries us across belongs to the 'old' world, a contraption of a wooden raft tied to a rusting boat with rope. An old, loud steam engine propels it across the waters at a leisurely pace. It is, unfortunately, Sunday—picnic day. A group of young women studying in a Christian teacher-training college merrily litter the waters with their plastic discharge. I intervene, meticulously trying to explain the properties of plastic. My lecture is met with derisive mocking laughter. Do I not know that water absorbs everything? To each other they say in Telegu: *Stupid foreigner!*

Even the boat is like a picnic ground. Families have brought huge food tiffins, chips, crunchies and timepass of all kinds. The debris is thrown into the waters.

Finally we reach the island. There is not much time to see

it. The site has been named a Buddhist site, but there are no stairs to its godowns. They are submerged in the depths of the water.

Many sculptures resist this Buddhist cataloguing, the oldest sculpture in particular. I am told it is two thousand years old. It is a huge sculpture of a squatting nude woman, with only the torso remaining. The head has disappeared. The original sculpture had no human head, but instead a lotus head symbolizing the figure of eight.

Headless Eros

sady-chinn-shirah-khadag-vam-urdhva-adhah-kar-ambujam
(The eternally cut head, the sword, the half-raised left hand)

—*Shaktpramod*

ambuja	=	arising from water
ambar	=	sky

One evening as Jamadagni's wife Renuka (grain, dust, pollen; the name of a well-known apsara) is bathing and washing her clothes, she sees her own reflection. The memory of the erotic play of the apsaras, the water goddesses, overwhelms her. Immersed in the sensuousness of her own eros, she returns home late. Her jealous husband orders his sons to behead her, but all of his sons except one refuse. Those who refuse are turned into dust, whilst Parsuram (Ram with the Axe) rapes and beheads Renuka. Terrified of his act, he tries to forget it, but each time he tries to bathe in the river its waters turn into blood. He beseeches his mother to come back to life, but she refuses to occupy her former role. Renuka becomes the headless

91

one, the one with the lotus head—an erotic memory—she returns to the waters. She becomes a lake.

Further south on the river, I visit another site, Alampur, that faced almost the same fate as Nagarjunkond. Some good sense prevailed, however; Alampur was only partially drowned. The walls of the dam now appear to enclose the temple landscape, form its boundary; the banks of the river are no longer visible. The course of the river has changed. Some temples are under the jurisdiction of the Archaeological Survey, and these are locked up. There are few visitors here, unlike the 'living temples' under the brahmin trust. They are as old as the other temples but have been sacrificed to the macabre kitsch of a certain modernity. A strange contrast between the One 'dead' and the One 'living'; time held silently still in red sandstone whereas the other blares its loudspeakers amidst its recently plastered blue, green, white and pink walls.

I visit the Alampur museum. Goddesses abound: Chamunda, Kali, Maheshasurmardini, the matrikas . . . they are all here, but Renuka is absent. I ask after her. The guard reluctantly unlocks a door to a tiny, dingy room and there she lies, immaculately preserved, on the floor. A millennium or two has gone by.

There is another sculpture, he says. It is in the living, so-called Brahma temple. As I enter this complex, I am greeted by an insistent group of widows with clean-shaven heads, voraciously demanding alms. They are like a living parody of Renuka.

Not only are the sandstone pillars whitewashed, but the temple's carvings have disappeared under multi-coloured dirt-smeared plaster. The earth, rust-red, has disappeared like the riverbanks.

Urdhva Tandav, dance of the skies,
approx. 7th century CE, (replica).

Dual chola bronze, approx. 7th century CE, (replica).

Reptile-headed yogini,
8th to 9th century CE,
Ranipur Jharial Orissa.

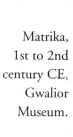
Matrika,
1st to 2nd
century CE,
Gwalior
Museum.

Bhadra Kali, the fierce kali, bronze,
17th century CE, Gwalior Museum.

Kunzamdevi, Kunzam Pass.

Dual, Konarak,
Orissa.

Yogini temple, 8th to 9th century CE,
Ranipur Jharial, Orissa.

Yogini temple, no exact dating, Dudhai.

Hermaphrodite Devi
pillar, 7th to 8th
century CE,
squatted on by a shop,
Kanchipuram.

Betwa River, Deogadh. Rock-cut temple situated nearby.

Rock-cut Matrika temple, 2nd to 4th century CE,
Deogadh, on the Betwa river.

Gyno-androus
Devi (goddess),
8th to 11th
century CE,
Gwalior
Museum.

Kundalini S-trip, Devi temple,
8th to 10th century CE, Darasuram Tamil Nadu.

Musical scene, 1st to 2nd century CE, Mathura Museum.

A young brahmin approaches me. I am a prospective client, after all. I ask to see Renuka, and again I am led to a small niche in one of the whitewashed corners. There is a small, dark underground chamber, barred and locked. Open sesame—and again, she lies on the floor. The figure is badly desecrated, her features despoiled by murky oils and her yoni smeared by hands guided by violent repressed fantasies.

I ask about the matricide myth, knowing fully well the answer that awaits me.

That was a mistake. Jamdagni, the brahmin rishi, brought her back to life. Renuka is our mother—barren women come to ask for her blessings to make their womb fecund.

I emerge from the vault and am again besieged by the widows. Not a paisa, I mutter. Go ask your brahmin babus.

I go to the now-centralized temple. It is known as the nav (new, nine) brahma temple. It is dark, and predictably there is a central figure—bedecked in gold. I look at the other niches. Some are empty; some have new sculpture. I go into a side room, and there sit the older figures—the matrikas. I video. No, no, no video, says the brahmin. This secret is not to be revealed—Chamunda will get angry.

The Chamunda in me starts to erupt. I continue to video. He changes his tactics: The head pandit will get angry!

In another dark room sits a mutilated figure of Chamunda. She is the wrath of Kali, the wrath of Renuka. It is a shaktic site, the brahmin acknowledges, which is why it needs so many brahmins to oversee it.

The pandits are like mullahs, but more fearful of the wrath (of Kali) that awaits them. Hence, with the left hand they try to appease Chamunda, keeping her arani (sacred firewood) secretly alive, while with the right hand they observe the law of the 'fathers'. It is a complex arithmetic, keeping the left hand, the vama, concealed, keeping down its numbers while increasing mass production on the right.

Mast Kalandar

> Happiness, the moment in which we are seated, I and you,
> in the palace, two figures, two forms, one spirit
>
> You and I
>
> The water/wine of life gives an immortal life to the saki,
> to the songs of the birds as we loiter together in the garden
>
> You and I
>
> The constellation of stars descends to observe us
> and the splendidness of our moon reveals itself to theirs
>
> You and I
>
> You and I without being You and I, flowing in ecstasy
> fused and joyous, free from all sheaths
>
> You and I
>
> Strange that you and I interwoven in one nest
> are in this moment in Iraq and Khorassan
>
> You and I
>
> —Rumi, *Diwan-e-Shams-e-Tabrizi*

The poetry of Rumi is alive. His love for his yaar, his friend, his beloved Shamsu, is sung repeatedly by the qawaals. Shamsu is his khuda, his god and his self (khud). Legends abound describing (t)his divine passion.

Rumi is a devout Muslim belonging to the tradition of the Right. He is righteous, and has forbidden the decadent jam-wine of the saki. Yet he is curious about the frenzy of the other half.

Shamsu arrives. He throws the Koran into the water. Rumi is horrified.

Shamsu says, What is a book worth? My khuda is a moment of complete masti, ecstasy with you.

A festival is to take place, seven days and seven nights long. Rumi is sent to get jam. He hides the bottles, but they fall out in the marketplace. He fetches them again, and this time he does not hide them.

> Give me the jam of your gaze . . .
> Give me the key to the mehkhana [godown].
> I am going to drink.

> —Qawaali, as performed by
> Nusrat Fateh Ali Khan

The festival starts. The music crescendoes to the spiralling dancing. The jaam overflows. Rumi forgets everything in the fullness of the masti.

> Dil rakh diya, sir rakh diya . . .
> I have placed my heart, my head . . .

Take me, he says to Shamsu as the festival ends.

The other side demands its revenge. Shamsu's head is axed. Rumi is inconsolable. His exile has begun; he wanders from place to place. Finally he sees Shamsu atop a minaret. He climbs up, but Shamsu is now below—dancing, holding his head in his left hand. Seven times Rumi goes up and down, but still Shamsu eludes him. Finally he throws himself down from the minaret, saying, 'Take me'.

Shamsu continues to dance, holding his head with his left hand and Rumi with his right.

Alampur to Hampi

I coast on the National Highway, the one that goes all the way to the land's tip, Kanyakumari—the immaculate Kumari, Kali with her three breasts and three eyes intact. This is the point where the three waters meet, the Bay of Bengal, the Arabian Sea and the Indian Ocean. I could reach it from here in two long days, but my route is serpentine—it follows the road and the river. The river takes me away from the sea into the interior of the land mass. I leave the National Highway and head towards Hampi, the ancient city of Vijaynagar.

The road is in a shambles and gets progressively worse. I reach Hampi in a state of collapsed shock and I lapse into fatigued sleep.

Faint blurred images. I struggle to attain focus. The images slowly become distinct. I am walking aimlessly. I follow a track that descends into a grove. There is an underground lake, a kund, with small temple shrines around it. Women are swimming in its transparent waters. I take my clothes off. I swim.

A strange, beautiful dream. I am not a good swimmer. This is the first time I have dreamt of swimming.

I amble through the ruins of Hampi. The site has changed since the last time I was here, over a decade ago. There were hardly any cafes, hardly any guest houses, hardly any people; just the bareness of the preserved ruins, the overwhelming presence of empty temples strewn in all directions. Cheap guest houses and cafes now abound, catering mainly to the leftover hippie generation and the new Israeli tourists who make their way from Goa. Busloads of young men from neighbouring villages, hurling sexist obscenities, periodically come for a women-ogling outing. New roads have been constructed, making it possible to drive to the temples, and the site has protected status now—it is a World Heritage Site under the aegis of UNESCO.

I walk about the main bazaar road and turn into a side alley. I am astounded by the image that greets me, though it takes me a while to gain clarity. There is a kund, around which are strewn small temple shrines.

I do not remember this place at all, although I had meticulously combed the ruins during my last visit, extensively photographing them not only with my camera but also with my memoric lens. Yet, while the topographic outlay somewhat matches that of my dreamscape, it is a mockery of its vision. The water of this kund is anything but clear; it is a dirty green filled with sewage and plastic. Some of the temples are white-washed, some used as garbage heaps, some occupied by squatters and some taken over by banana plantations. They are all Devi shrines, with the customary iconographic signature of one form of Kali and one of Gaj-Lakshmi. Here, Laksmi sits on a lotus flanked by two elephants. Clothes hang in some of her shrines, a stray dog scrounges the garbage heaps for its daily meal, and sculptures lie amidst a burst water pipe. All white-washed, they are serpentine figures, some with female heads. Their style suggests they are the oldest sculptural remains in Hampi. Chamunda is among them, but with a serpentine body.

Horror and exhilaration flood me simultaneously. Wonder gives way to a surreal, macabre theatre of rot.

To escape, I plunge into the waters of a dreamscape recounted to me by a woman in a workshop in Himachal Pradesh:

> I am walking through a village. I come across a pool of water. Its waters are shallow and unclear. I walk further and see another pool of water. Its waters are translucent. A man is sitting by the wayside. He says to me: These waters are dangerous. Bathe in the other pool. It is safe there.
>
> I look at the other pool. It does not attract me. I jump in the deep lake. I start to sink. I sink deeper and deeper. Suddenly I start to rise, buoyantly, up to the surface again. A woman is holding me. I float in her hands. I float in the waters.

I go to the local museum and seek a meeting with the archaeological in-charge. He tells me that this particular part of the site is not under ASI's jurisdiction; it is under that of the state department of archaeology, who in turn have turned it over to the brahmin trust of the living temple.

But surely something can be done? I ask. This is a World Heritage Site. These shrines must be protected. They are intrinsic to the site. They constitute the oldest part!

I insist emphatically but politely, knowing full well that this conversation is as futile as my earlier fight with the brahmin pandit.

Madam, you know how it is here. Look how much we have done for the temples that are under us. See how we have made the gardens around them.

He shows me some photographs. The contrast is striking, an illustration of a recurring phenomenon: One part of the site is idyllically preserved, the other a reflection of living rot. The third part must be ignored, consigned to:

Familiar Oblivion

I walk through the crowded bazaar, struggling to avoid the people, the animals, the lecherous looks. I hurry to reach my room and discharge the heavy burden of my camera bag. There is an old Devi temple somewhere nearby, but for the moment I am not sure I want to wade through its rot to find the rainbow at the other end of its tunnel.

The light is now changing, the sun slowly withdrawing her intensity, the rays of Ushas bedecking the stones with a golden-red sheen. The temple is on my route—a familiar path, a path I have trod often. A man stands at the corner and says something inaudible. We get into an altercation. He hesitantly beckons me inside the temple.

I step in. The man is relieved; it is as though he has been waiting for me. It is a Chamunda temple. There are two main icons diagonally facing each other. Both are three-headed matrikas, one Chamunda and the other Varahi, the matrika with the boar's head. The head on the left side of Varahi is talking to the head on the right side of Chamunda. The mouths move, but no sound is audible. In disbelief, I say to the man: There is no sound.

The man is astonished. I should know better, being an initiate.

I make the switch from the limited to the other known consciousness. The conversation takes place in silence. The evening light is beautiful, dusk in all of its splendour. Should I photograph? I am carrying my camera equipment, but the light is not sufficient for the image that I want to bring out. I can always access this reality, so why photograph? I will wait till the light is perfect. This is part of the everyday, after all.

Is my external pilgrimage no other than a Moebius strip where one side unfolds the other, where inner and outer differences collapse in the realm of uncanny dreams that elude rational explication? To even attempt to decipher such dreams would be to lose their melodic thread.

Is my journey the search for a musical composition complex and yet so minimal, where the notes played by the left and the right hands perform a strange dance on the piano, creating a sonic tapestry, the intersection of memoric, dream and waking landscapes, audible and inaudible?

Conflicting Theologies

The river Tungabhadra, another part of the Krishna, flows in the vicinity. A huge dam has been built on this section, but it has not submerged Hampi. Historic ruins are scattered in all directions. Rock-cut caves, majestic sandstone sculptures and small shrines depicting numerous cosmologies seem to have been part of the river's surrounding landscapes. The presence of Renuka graces many of these sites. Like the curvaceous river, the temples, too, seem to have followed a winding path.

How did one find these sites when they were alive, when their traditions flourished? What was the nature of travel then, the nature of pilgrimage? It seems impossible even to speculate on these questions. The boundaries are drawn; a frontier is clearly marked between the worlds that generated these cosmologies and my path, which traces the routes of their ruins as I seek to excavate their memories from the debris of destruction.

Even my compulsions I am not able to rationalize. What are the cosmological questions that propel *me*, that compel me to take on the role of a wandering philosopher? Is it not only the retracing of lost time, but also the unfolding of the labyrinthine nature of my own route that kindles this passion?

My first lucid memory of theological enquiry dates from when I was a child of six, debating the existence of a god. The concept appeared inadequate to answer the mystery of existence. In retrospect, the question I seemed to be asking was one of cosmological existentialism: Is our existence simply a state from which we pose the question of other forms of existence? Is it by delving into the 'unknown' and contemplating its wondrousness that we seek a revelation of our own existence, our own khuda, our own maya?

> *aham guptakarah sthithah tatah prasidhah syam-iti-icchaya srishti kritvani-iti*
>
> *tasya mayayah sakashat jivatma pradurbabhuv*
>
> I, the hidden form exists; this is established. Through desire is enacted creation,
>
> through whose maya is manifested and made visible the essence/soul/breath of materiality.
>
> —Cited by Dara Shukhoh
> in *Samudrasangam*

Dara Shukhoh was the eldest son of the Mughal emperor Shah Jahan, and the rightful successor to his throne. Though he was fluent mainly in Persian and Arabic, he wrote the above text in Sanskrit; he sought to establish philosophical and cosmological connections between these cultural and linguistic traditions. Perhaps he envisioned himself as an intellectual mediator, a trader, like those who had moved between southern and central Asia before the advent of the holy wars, the hegemony of divine belief.

Allah become one of the hegemony's divine singular nominations, Arabic its official sacred language. Allat, its feminine predecessor, khuda, its Persian other, got buried along the way. Dara, too, lost this war, lost his maya, his khuda, to his younger brother's Allah. Like Abel, slain by Cain, he was brutally murdered in public by his brother—a terrible crime that seems to have a long history. How many mystics, fakirs, witches, dakins, 'unbelievers' and shaitans have been killed by the fear generated by confrontation with theological doubt? Was not the revelation of one's maya a much more complex form of the unravelling of one's psyche?

The word *psyche* has its origin in the Greek word *pséchein*, which means 'breath' and hence 'life'. In mythology, it takes the form of a beautiful girl loved by Eros. In other words, the psyche is the animating, pulsating energy of desire. At an abstract and philosophical level, it connotes the ensemble of psychic forces that make up an individual. Another early meaning was that of a grand, mobile mirror.

Is khuda nothing more than a form of narcissistic reflection? Is its enjoyment merely its revelation? If so, who needs the revelations of the prophets, the messiahs, the clergy, the mullahs, the pandits? Who needs their brokers and middlemen? Why wait eternally for Godot?

My first confrontation with this fear came during my school days. I was sent to a convent school, a residual remnant of Catholic colonialism. Convent schools were seen then, and are still somewhat seen now, as the haven of Indian girls' education.

A marriage advertisement that never fails to lighten my mood has the following description: Brahmin homely girl, convented, wheatish complexion . . .

We followed in the footsteps of our mothers, most of whom had also been 'convented'. I got constantly into trouble. The first inquisition came about when I was eight. I had not done my homework. Instead of making an excuse, I simply stated the truth—the homework bored me. This innocuous statement, made in complete naivete, was like inadvertently dropping a bombshell. I was called to the staff quarters, where all the teachers there were informed of my misdeed and asked to condemn the Satan in me. Only one of the teachers gently had the last word:

At least she spoke the truth.

The climax followed a few years later. One of the things I detested most about school was attending assembly, for which we had to line up early in the morning and have our uniforms checked by the school prefects. We wore white skirts, white blouses and white shoes, all of which had to be completely and spotlessly white, especially the shoes—not an easy task in a dusty country like India. Every day, there was a regular theatre of girls looking for white chalk to lighten the dark spots on their shoes.

Our belts were red, and we were supposed to tie our hair with a red ribbon or band. I refused to wear anything in my hair. It was too short for a ribbon anyway, and a hairband gave me a headache. As for assembly, who wanted to stand in a straight line and recite day after day the same absurd lines, over and over again?

Our father, who art in heaven / Holy be thy name . . .

To avoid the daily conflict, I stopped attending assembly. Usually the prefects left me in peace when they were sent on their hunt; they preferred to have their peace as well. But one time, a prefect insisted. She called the teacher in charge.

Some girls are very stupid, said the teacher.

In my opinion, I replied, stupidness lies elsewhere.

Before I knew it, I received a tight slap across my face.

I burst out laughing.

I was taken straight to the principal, the Head Mother. She was the first Indian to be accorded this position, having taking over from a British and Irish lineage. An apology was demanded of me, but I refused to make it. For over a month, I was called every day to the Head Mother's office for a theological discussion.

What do you have against assembly? she said. Praying is holy.

I don't like praying, I said. Besides, I do not believe in Jesus.

You have no place in our school if you do not believe in God.

Books were holy to me. I had just read *The Brothers Karamazov* and been profoundly affected by Ivan's statement that God is a creation of man. I articulated my argument in all good faith, and the Head Mother listened and argued back in turn. The arguments did break my daily monotony; and, relief of reliefs, I was exempted from attending assembly on the grounds that I had no belief. The end of the conversation, however, was always the same.

Have you decided to apologize? If you don't, we will have no choice but to expel you.

A month or two later, I dropped out of school.

Out of Hampi, out of its ruins, out of its timescape, I arrive at the junction town of Hospet. The bumpy, potholed road comes to an end here, but I still have to drive out of this repulsive town to access the National Highway. The small link roads are a disaster for my accident-battered neck and spine, so I try to stay on the highways that connect the major cities.

Hospet is is no different from any other town I have driven through; its infrastructure is in a state of collapse. Two main roads cut across it, but one is being dug up because a sewage pipe has burst. The squalor is in sharp contrast to the open skies and seemingly endless fields of crops I have left behind. It elicits the same reaction in me that all small towns elicit—shut down all senses, drive away as soon as possible and keep the eyes focussed on the road.

Out of Hospet, out of the road-construction area, I slowly reactivate my senses. There is little traffic, and the road gets progressively smoother as urban modernity approaches. Then the traffic increases. It is time to stop, to get my jeep checked and spruced up.

Bangalore is meant to be the electronic capital of India, the national computer haven, and it has a quality of freshness I have never otherwise experienced in an Indian metropolis. Calcutta crumbles. Mumbai overwhelms, trying desperately from its limited space to stretch out to the sky, into the sea, into the land . . . it is a city bordered by chawls and pavement dwellers amidst a khichdi of Bollywood and the histrionics of its ex-helmsman, the failed cartoonist in orange. Hyderabad, or rather its twin city, Secunderabad, also aspires to modernity and electronic repute, but the twins, built on opposite sides of the river, embody the split and schizophrenia of different timescapes—the newer, planned urban colonies and the older, cloistered, cramped narrow enclosures. An image that repeatedly confronts me in the crowded Charminar bazaars aptly expresses this contrast: fresh, cool, white cotton kurta-pyjamas hanging on a clothes stand next to thick, heavy black burqas. Both swing merrily in the warm breeze of the stifling sun.

The birth of the modern Indian city is interwoven with the exit of the British and the advent of homegrown industry. I am a product of this phenomenon, a habitant of New Delhi—the capital, with its wide avenues and new colonies. The house in which now I live is only as old as I am, yet it is an 'ancestral' house handed down by my mother's parents—the crystallization of my grandmother's dream after her empty-handed flight from Lahore.

Bahut iksha thi ghar banane ki, lekin Daddy nahin chahte the.

I had a lot of desire to build a house, but your grandfather did not want it.

My grandmother's story is both typical and unique. Typical for the collective wound of displacement and the city's policy: Land was available for the asking. Many areas were half jungle, and needed to be urbanized; the city had to be created yet anew. It was no longer the capital of the English but belonged to the new India, free but partitioned. Delhi invited new immigrant refugees to participate in this project of making history, forging modernity.

But this story is unique because it was not the male householder who built a new home but rather my grandmother, a tiny woman barely four feet eight inches short, hardly educated, and married at the age of twelve. She commuted daily from the Chandni Chowk of Old Delhi, from north to south, the back of beyond at that time. She sought out an architect, hired a contractor, learnt all about building materials and techniques and went about the task of construction with her customary zeal and perfectionism, or her 'tiptop character', as she described it in her minimal English.

An old memory returns, an image surprisingly clear, of the house where my grandmother lived in Old Delhi. I must have been around two years old, for my great-grandmother was alive. This is the only memory I have of her—sitting on the charpoy in the house's inner courtyard, basking in the winter sun. It is this quality of sensuousness that has kept the image of the courtyard and my great-grandmother fresh in me.

The new house did not have an enclosed verandah, around which would have been various rooms typical of the traditional joint-family arrangement. Instead it had a large living room, bedrooms, attached bathrooms, an open garden and a marble tub, in whose cold water I spent many a summer afternoon.

I grew up in a similar house in the same colony. The colony itself was built around open parks and a marketplace; adjacent to it was another enclave with small, enclosed galis like those in an overgrown village. It had a facade of timber shops and car, scooter and motorcycle mechanics, while buffalos, cows, pigs, goats, donkeys and the like strolled within the galis.

The same house and shop that sold supposedly uncontaminated buffalo's milk also had a welding unit. The mingling of the new, open urban space with the village was counterpointed by old ruins, which still lay strewn all over.

A city that can at best be described as a maze that reflects the rises and ebbs of different civilizations, their elaborate palimpsest, even in its layers of different names: Indraprastha, Yoginipura, Dilli, Delhi, New Delhi and so forth. The bureaucratic city, the colonial city, the Mughal city, the temple city of Lalkot in its smashed remains, the groves and parks, the old ruined terraces where one could sit and watch peacocks and vultures, sinking away to memoric rapture under one's own hashish trip. Djinns and yoginis were said to have inhabited these fantastic realms.

The mechanic approaches to return my repaired jeep. He has kept his word—he has worked the entire morning on his day off to have my jeep ready. He has redone the suspension completely, changed all the axle bearings, fully serviced and generally spruced up the jeep. He is no longer in his mechanic clothes but is dressed in his Sunday best, mobile phone neatly tucked into his shirt pocket. He drives a new Korean car. It suddenly occurs to me that the mixture of professionalism and pleasantness that he embodies can also be said to belong to the city. Bangalore is unencumbered by centuries of history and devoid of the customary strolling stray cows on its large, tree-lined avenues. Its centre is filled with an assortment of shopping malls, Internet cafes, bars and multi-cuisine restaurants where beer and wine are no issue. It appears to be at ease with its modernity. Its newness is not displeasing, not a striking contrast, not a schizophrenic Other of an older reality.

I, too, feel fresh here. I am no longer a gender anomaly or a foreigner as I ask a young woman, dressed much as I am, the way to my hotel. After the weeks of being in villages and small towns where the public presence of women is rare, Bangalore is like an idyll. To see women on the streets, not to have to confront constant voyeuristic invasion! Theatre, good food, no blaring loudspeakers in the small cafes . . . instead, quiet garden terraces and a charming gay friend and escort are only some of the luxuries the city seems to offer. As I walk through the public garden, the fragrance of the flowers in bloom wafts through me.

Several years ago, in transit in Raipur, a small town in Madhya Pradesh near the border of Orissa, we waited for the flight that would take us back to Delhi. We had just completed a long journey to Orissa's yogini sites. To pass time, we wandered through the maze of small shops. My friend suddenly remembered the incense she was supposed to take back to a friend in Europe. We enquired in several shops and got the same message from each: There was one shop that would certainly have what we required. Step by step, we were guided there.

I had no nose for incense. Till then, it had belonged to another world—that of dirty temples and Western notions of Indian exotica. Yet the moment I stepped into this shop, I stepped over my own prejudicial threshold. It was tiny, but it overflowed with different kinds of incense sticks. The owner explained and demonstrated the different kinds of perfumes. Aroma after aroma wondrously seduced us into another world, initiating us into a cosmos of scents. Each fragrance had its own entity, its own peculiarity, just as in my childhood each rose had had its own scent, its own name and its own colour composition. Ittar, jasmine, sandalwood, raat ki rani . . . these incense sticks were a very subtle combination of many different woods and flowers. Others were minimal, useful in keeping away certain kinds of insects. Some sticks were expensive, while others were discounted for those who had little money. Our friend's philosophy: Everyone should be able to enter this world.

I asked him whether it was a family business; he said no. So how did the shop emerge?

He had grown up in Raipur. His family had sent him to Bangalore to study engineering. As he was jogging through the public garden in Bangalore, he became aware of the scents of the plants and flowers around him. He gave up engineering, returned to Raipur and started a flower business.

I was surprised. Somehow I had always thought of the flower business as a new phenomenon. The rose garden in my father's factory was purely his pleasure, and the flowers in our house always came from our gardens. The practice of buying flowers in a shop was one I associated with the new cities, the new middle classes and the nouveau riche.

He explained that there had been an aristocratic clientele then. Slowly this class grew poorer, lost their earlier glory and became a dwindling reality. It was then that our friend had the idea of transforming the world of flowers into that of their scents—the world of incense sticks, scented oils and perfumes would give him greater variety. He could now develop his own art, mix his own perfumes, create new odours, generate another connaissance: a philosophical ethos of sugandh.

Agar andar sugandh hai, to bahar klesh nahin hota.

If there is a fragrance inside, there is no conflict outside.

A simple philosophy, lucid and clear. Fragrant.

Leftover Turning Points

Back on the road again. Each stop brings me further to my destination—the land's end. The density of population seems to increase as the lands starts to get narrower. The sea gets closer. I cross the border into Tamil Nadu and head towards my next destination: Kanchipuram, a town known for its abundance of old temples. A decade ago I was astounded by encounters with sculpture everywhere in Kanchipuram, be it in the chowk, a small new factory or an old house. Much of it has been whitewashed now, 'modernized'; in the chowk, hoardings have been pasted over some of the sculptures. One exquisite hermaphrodite figure has rope tied around and over it. The town seems much more crowded and aggressive. The contrast after Bangalore is crass, one's cosmopolitan pleasantness in sharp cacophony to the other's blaring temple loudspeakers.

The Tamil Nadu Tourism guest house is supposedly full; only rooms in the top category are available. I take one without a second thought. Some political VVIP is making his temple rounds, and his entire entourage is here along with masses of security police. The room is large—must have been part of an older, more stylish bungalow—but now has an unkempt feel, complete with peeling paint. Mosquitoes are rampant, and the electric repellent does not work. Fortunately I have my own, one of the few travel contraptions I find indispensable. The food in the adjoining cafe is equally repellent, but the room is quiet, perhaps the only quiet area in this silence-forsaken town. One can hear birds, and to my wonder I even glimpse a golden oriole.

The experience of wonder is soon over. The visit to the temples is disastrous. The Kamakshi temple, which I photographed a decade ago, is a caricature of its older self. Many of the sculptures no longer exist; they have been plastered over. All that remains of the iconography is a series of grey lumps. One of the open sanctums has a network of grilles within it, and the sculptures are covered by huge, framed, garlanded photographs of 'holy' men, one more obese than the other. Another part of the temple is used as the pandits' living quarters. Clothes hang from the pillars, and an elephant is led inside to be decorated for the evening tamasha. I do not even have the energy to photograph. It has taken only ten years of free India to erase what existed for over a thousand years. No outside invasion was needed.

The sanctums were originally called sahasr mandap, thousand-pillar sanctums. They were like a complex film script, as the visuals could move in the many directions of one's gaze—top to bottom, bottom to top, left to right, right to left, spirally, diagonally. The intricacy of darshan, their visual experience, was endless.

Darshan kar lo, darshan darshan do rupaya mai darshan kara denge!

Two rupees for a round of darshan, shout the pandits.

Puri's Jagannath temple is one of the most prestigious living temples, and easily one of the dirtiest. Only the 'purest' Hindus are allowed inside. Even Indira Gandhi was not granted access, as she was married to a non-Hindu—a Parsi.

I politely refuse the offer of darshan and reply that I would prefer to do my own sv-darshan (self-darshan). One pandit starts to stick to me, worse than a leech. First he offers to bring down his price. When this does not work, he gets aggressive. I get equally aggressive—I tell him that if he had any sacred sense he would realize that people need to be left alone, in peaceful silence. This heritage is no one's property, and what does he know of the place, anyway? I ask him if he knows Sanskrit. I repeat the question in Sanskrit.

He says: Don't let her go inside. She is a Muslim.

The destruction of older temples and sculptures by Islamic invaders is an indelible historical fact; it belongs to the theological will to power. It is the war of that will. But this living destruction is beyond any rational or aesthetic understanding. The more extreme the alienation, the more glorious its expression of foul kitsch.

A kitsch that purely stinks.

Imaginary Sanctuaries

I escape the putrid kitsch and head towards the bird sanctuary recommended by the guidebooks. It appears to be close by, and lodging is indicated. I have in mind a comfortable drive, an hour, perhaps. The road should be in good condition— I have driven on it before—and perhaps I will see some more golden orioles. The thought of staying two or three days in a beautiful wetland in the sonic space/-scape of bird calls is *onirique*, dreamlike. Even the thought that it will delay the sight of the sea is not displeasing.

The road is in tatters. Still, I think, sixty kilometres is not much, and the road will surely get better at the next turnoff point. I count the kilometres yet try to relish the small villages, the occasional river tributary and the lotus ponds. The highways are not crowded, and there is much to see beyond the next pothole. My mood still holds, and the jeep has been freshly repaired.

113

The turnoff point comes, but the next road is in the same condition. Unfathomable—I have somehow always assumed that the south is better linked, more efficient in these matters, cleaner. Later, when I revisit this area the roads have been repaired. The nine-month difference is due to the change of government, the hired driver explains to me in his bricoleur English.

Terrible roads, Madam. Last year big rain; roads all washed. Amma not interested in repairing. First thing new government do—make roads.

Amma, or Jayalalithaa, and her government probably spent the state's resources elsewhere, but thankfully the political shift brought about a road shift. This is partly for political convenience, of course; the ruling politicians need to travel comfortably, and not just on the highways. Did Amma not visit the interiors?

My cousin once told me about a road in Assam of which each of the two main political parties maintained half. When there was a power shift, the half of the road that was in good shape was deliberately allowed to deteriorate, whereas the part in shambles was made into a flying carpet. At no point was the road completely driveable; it was always a question of which half.

The main road comes and is considerably better, but now the signs are only in Tamil. I ask directions, but most people do not know what a bird sanctuary is, and English is a foreign language. Hindi is not even worth trying. I go up and down the road, wondering who in this rural area will know some English. The link language is missing, perhaps symbolizing the link road to the sanctuary. I look around for someone who might be a local teacher, and finally I do find someone who carefully and precisely delineates the route.

I arrive to find a small pool of water. There are not many birds, just the waterfowl that one finds in any rural water body. I spot an abandoned house. Could this be the resthouse? The rest of the area is entirely cultivated.

I turn around, retrace the tattered road and reach the next site after a few hours of battered body and shattered mood. This site is one of those discoveries that I owe partly to chance and partly to research. I once lingered in Pondicherry—time seemed to be standing still—and a whim took me to the French Indological Institute. To my amazement, I found a catalogue of photographs of an assortment of temple sculptures. The photos were taken mainly in the fifties, and each was dated and carried a description of the site. It was a treasure trove. The photos that particularly struck me came from a site called Devikapuram, a name that is not Tamil but Sanskrit: City of the Goddess. It intrigued me. The next day I hired a taxi and found it in a remote village. No one questioned my presence, and in a state of bliss I feasted on the rows of feminine sculpture, photographing to my heart's content.

I feel I cannot leave this area without returning to Devikapuram, despite knowing what kind of road awaits me. I drive through. Not much has changed since my last visit. Even then, a certain amount of manipulative kitsch was visible, and a small shrine was used as the living quarters of a cow and an old man, the latter of whom sat staring away into space. The cow dung seems to lie exactly as I saw it earlier, and the huge wasp hives at the temple's entrance hang down in the same way.

One of the sanctums is used as a storeroom, its ceiling painted green and orange, but the sculptures have not been destroyed. Even in the main sanctum no further damage seems to have been done, though a massive Shiv-Parvati poster has been pasted over some pillars. Some other garlanded calendar photographs have been suspended over a row of dancing women intertwined in each other. The contrast, as usual, is ludicrous.

Yet the magical spell that the site casts upon me remains unchanged. The brief time that I spend here overcomes my fatigue and hunger. It seems to me that I belong here, that I have my continuum here, that I am neither in exile nor a foreigner despite my present problem of not speaking Tamil. This is a known place. Its vitality is somehow intact and seems to affirm me in my own, as if the erotic feminine presence is as much in the stone sculptures as in me and my darshan.

It is four p.m. and I have to drive another 150 kilometres. Part of it, again, is in tatters. Luckily it is the first part, and the few remaining hours of daylight will allow me to circumvent some of the potholes. A drive that should have been sixty kilometres long—from Kanchipuram to the bird sanctuary— has become 460; what should have taken one hour has taken ten. Yet as I finish it and find a hotel facing the Bay of Bengal, the starlit sea, there is the feeling of having arrived, or, rather, in the words of V.S. Naipaul:

The Enigma of Arrival

Any journey to the sea is traced out through land. In some senses the routes are marked—by maps, by roads—so it is not that one charts out the unknown. On the contrary, it is no major feat to approach the sea; a triviality. Yet after these long days of driving, changing landscapes, changing timescapes, changing seasons, changing cosmologies, changing languages— so much movement—perhaps the experience of enigma is in what appears trivial. To straddle its multiplicities—to be in and out of its realities—for each has its reality—there is no fiction in this logic. The reality of one's thoughts, the reality of one's dreams—the detail in the constantly changing flux. As if each drop in the sea has its own reality, is microcosmic, though in its movement—in its flow, in its flux—it appears formless, ever-changing. Its element, water, does not have the demarcations that land has. Land is the threshold of water as water is the threshold of land, in its encompassing expansiveness. It is light that marks the water, light that colours it, allowing it to reflect—it *is* the reflection—becoming a mirror.

> She, the sum of all the infinite forms
>   the first, carrier/generatrice of the self form
>   spread through the liminal intelligence [chit]
> At one time, Shiva perceived her own reflection
> Then the reflection became Maya, thus the abstract shiv
> To know the meaning of creation, contemplate the
>   bearing-generative form
> To know the first genders of adi-nath, and manasa,
>   contemplate in extreme the self-form
> She, enacting the inverted feminine eros [viprit rati]
>   in the mode of the great void [maha shunya],
>   the three-part serpent-foetus, the six circles, then the
>   cave of the lotus
> For centuries there existed the inverted feminine eros
> The goddess amidst the inverted eros becomes the micro-
>   cosmic point

Thus emerges the One, the beautiful woman from
  the great ocean
Kalika, the beautiful form of the woman,
  the carrier of the first part
She of the abstract feminine energy emerging
  from the beyond of the beyond
  nominated Mahakali,
  the contemplation of the form of the beautiful woman

—Kali Khand,
Shakti-Sangam Tantra

Is the enigma of arrival no other than the enigma of birth?

Over the Threshold

After a sound, dreamless sleep, I awake to the sound of waves
and a vision of brilliant red light on the sea. I observe the sun
gradually emerge from within the waters. The view of the sea
and the rhythmic sounds of its waters are restful. It seems a
strange continuation of my last night in Pondicherry, nine
years ago.

It has taken me nine years to return to Pondicherry, and this
is still not really Pondicherry; it is a seafront hotel about twelve
kilometres away. In fact, I am not quite sure whether it belongs
to Tamil Nadu or to Pondicherry. Last time I stayed in the town
itself, in a cheap guest house; and in the early morning I was
greeted not by the amazing symphony of colour on an expanse
of water, but rather by a view of pavement dwellers expressing
their frustrations through raucous shouting, almost as if to
challenge the ashram-seekers' desire for stillness and meditation.

The main attraction in Pondicherry was and remains the

ashram, an experiment that arose amidst the backdrop of French colonial architecture. The French language brought its two founders together: Aurobindo, a brahmin from Bengal, and the 'Mother', of mixed Arabic and French origin. Together they decided to form an international community. As is often the case when parents die, the offspring moved in several directions and squabbled over their heritage. A split came about and the international facade gave way to bitter fights, more often than not ethnically grounded.

The town and the ashram, with its huge photographs of Mother and Father Aurobindo everywhere, unsettled me. The cheap fare in the ashram was good for the pocket—for Rs 10 you could eat three times a day—but it had no spices whatsoever, and garlic was strictly taboo. There was plentiful bland porridge for breakfast, lunch and dinner. I grew restless and frenzied, and it was then that I discovered the French Indological Institute and Devikapuram.

After that visit, I had meant to travel on to Kanyakumari. Now, I am looking forward to my next stop, Chidambaram, which eluded me on my earlier trip.

Coincidence: in German, *zufall* (falling to). A concurrence of events, an event simply falling to one. A crossroads, perhaps, or a roundabout. I have come around but not quite back to this point, a little ahead. But the to-and-fro nature of the route is *boulversant*.

And this little ahead is not the confinement of the town, its confining and complex ashram culture, its decrepit yet aesthetic French colonial architecture. It is not to this point that I have returned, but to that next point in my earlier journey.

The frenzy has given over to the serenity of the sea.

Gateway to the Liminal Sky

Chidambaram—the chit-ambar, the liminal intelligence/ consciousness of the skies. The English translation is ponderous compared to the playfulness of the Sanskrit compound word. *Chit* denotes a state in which the process of becoming conscious of a phenomenon is equated to liminal/luminal intelligence.

This time the journey to Chidambaram is hazard-free. In slightly over an hour I reach the temple. It is a gigantic complex in the form of an open rectangle to which four portals, dvars, invite entry. Amidst an array of temples, old and new, forming part of the central space, is a huge kund containing stagnant, mossy water. Beggars at each portal tug away at my shirt, making their pitiful demands. When these go unheard, laments rapidly change to aggressive insults.

Chidambaram is known as a dance site: the place where Shiv defeated Kali in a dance contest. It was a stiff competition, we are repeatedly told by priests, Indologists and anthropologists. Each mudra, each gesture, each position, each movement was evenly matched. When the contest reached its climax, its moment of decision, Shiv raised his right leg at a stiff angle to begin his dance of death—the urdhva tandav.

A cloud of shame overcame Kali. She suddenly became a shy, demure damsel. How could she raise her leg and open her yoni to the sky? The dance was over, the vanquisher's lordship clearly established.

The story intrigues me. Why was this particular mudra, this movement, so important? What lay behind its taboo? It compels me to start looking at iconographies of dance, its symbolic implications. Soon I have a small collection. I find the iconography in many different epochs and geographies, even on a modern postcard depicting a woman Bharatnatyam dancer enacting this mudra.

North India, Nepal, the high Himalayas, the merusthal, the land of Mount Meru—Kali takes on a range of dancing avatars known as the dakinins and the vajr yoginis. This mudra is only one movement in a sequence—in the flourish of one stroke, the expanse of the skies becomes their dancing abode. This is a dance of the mountains, the dance of their rooftops.

But the myth of the dance contest comes from the south. And Chidambaram is near the sea, its surrounding landscapes overflowing with estuaries and mangroves. Was this site crucial to the establishment of Nordic brahminic hegemony? What did Kali's epithets symbolize?—Maha Dakshina Kalika, the Great Kali of the South; Maha Shunya, Maha Pralay-Nama.

None of the iconographies in my collection is identical to its male counterpart. The angle of the raised leg is not stiff. One of my first discoveries was a rare replica of a Tamil bronze in which the raised leg is not held away from the body like the man's but is graciously curved, culminating in the foot touching the head. It is as if the movement draws its source from the yoni, opens its energy and channels it into a curvaceous flow that leads to the chakra on the head. Meanwhile, a snake-like figure flows out from the yoni to the ground. The body appears a micro-cosmos, a chakra of spiralling energy—kundalini—that can flow in both directions.

Svechaya valyam kritva yatha kundalini stitha . . . sa-ardh tri vali devi

Enacting the auto-erotic, the serpentine Vali—thus the

establishing of the kundalini . . . she the in-between three-vali goddess

Maya-prakriti ev srishti-stithi-lay

The movement from maya to prakriti enacts the three-fold state of the goddess, of creation, maintenance and dissolution into dynamic energy.

—*Kali Tantra*

I have already seen many individuated manifestations of the Kali-tandav during my earlier travels in the south. Chidambaram should be no exception; research suggests it was a Kali site. But what awaits me at its dvars, at its doors, at its portals is an unimaginable explosion. I realize that all my thoughts have been conservative as I gaze at the poses and poses of dance—the tandav in so many forms—the leg at so many angles—so many curves, so many nuances—and not a single dancer is male. Not even the minute figures carved on the ceilings are male. Everywhere I look I see women dancers, single, fused and interlinked.

There is no evidence of a contest here. There is only an epiphany of dance.

Suktani tri-sahsrani tandavanam shatam shive

Shiva, she hundred-fold, of the chain of the three thousand forms of tandav, of transformative dance

The *Kali Tantra* is no invention, only meticulous description serving as a dvar to its darshan.

An epiphany of dance—appearance after appearance—mudra after mudra—lay after lay—rhythm after rhythm, sequence after sequence—the flow within, the flow without—

the opening of the yonic kundalini to the sky—flying into the skies—if the dakinis embody the dance of the roof of the world, the play of the mountains, Chit-ambar is the expansive consciousness of the celestial dance of the skies.

The roof of the world becomes reflected in the drops of the oceans as the sea touches the mountain in the great celestial dance.

I waltz into the skies.

The Dual, Inter-twin-ing

shadows as mirrors shadows as mirrors
reflecting glowing
without light the deep waters
my face luminescent
in darkness in darkness
in the cave in the well
enshrouded contained
the flower of Narcissus the self fires

immersed in the alchemy of fire-water

brilliant flames intersecting
into the rose of crossing paths

immersed in the alchemy of water-fire

vibrant red waves streaming
into the lotus of flowing isles

dark, the passing over, the birds,
carriers, robed in the waters,
ascending to the light
descending from the dwelling
moistening the earth with their fluids

the island floating in black gold droplets glistening over
the cloak woven by weaving stars englobing the cup

dark—the passing over—the barque crossing over
into the mist
hidden—the secret dwelling
revealing itself
in the
    mirror play
of the light twins

Grammars shape languages. They lay the archi-text-ural foundations for words, for their syntaxes and montages to evolve. They give form to wordless thoughts that circum-ambulate one's mind.

Before I discovered the pleasure of learning new languages and plumbing the labyrinths of their literatures, I felt that thoughts in silence, without body, were the foremost abstractions—only possible to touch through music, through the precision of mathematics. Numbers, real and imaginary, took me to another place. Their relationships were finely tuned as those of intervals between musical notes. A Bach fugue, the art of counterpoint, seemed to reflect the subtlest harmony that balanced the dissonant chaos of life, of its emotional and erotic turbulences. Music as the expression of a certain mathematics seemed to reflect the innate lyricism of emotions, of their dramaturgies, yet always with the potential of concordance.

Melody and Harmony

Numbers did not seem to be of much use in languages. The only mathematical differentiation seemed to be between the singular and the plural states. Yet when I started re-learning

Sanskrit as an adult, I was confronted not with chains of words that I had as a child memorized incessantly but that of another philosophy of numbers. Its grammar, in addition to the singular and the plural, had also the *dual*.

At first it appeared irrelevant. One could always prefix a noun with a two. Yet the more I came across the dual usage, I realized that it was not equivalent to simply stating two of a kind. Mathematically, two was a real number and a quantitative concretization; but the numerous dual usages in cosmologies, like those of dawn and light, seemed to lie beyond finite measurement. Something else lay concealed—an archaeological find, a mathematical puzzle to be solved, an enigma waiting to be revealed.

I mulled and mulled, but its/their mystery eluded me. As much as I tried my various keys, the lock refused to budge. Its door remained shut—an impasse—its travesty strictly out of bounds.

Yet the dual seemed to perpetually confront me. It gave me no peace, but repeated recurringly in all my findings. It took the form of pairs, twins, complements, supplements, reflections, equivalents, shadows, alter egos, and identical selves. As I aimlessly engaged in the game of timepass in a Tamil Nadu handicraft emporium to which I'd accompanied a friend, a small bronze sculpture tucked away in a corner caught my eye: two women dancers fused from the navel. Two separate upper bodies, but one common torso. I was allowed to photograph it, to record it, but it still lay outside my financial reach. Every once in a while I would return to the shop, and still the sculpture would await me. After over five years of visiting it, I finally took it home. I celebrated 'their' arrival. I gave it/them

125

the choicest shelf, the best light. The key started to move, yet the lock lay firmly clasped.

Here in Chidambaram, amidst the piles of rubbish, a chain of sculptures, even more minute in size, carved on the base of the temples, seems to beckon me. They appear to be older than their larger counterparts, which are chiselled on the upper levels of pillars. But many of these pillars have received another coat of time. Distemper has conveniently veiled the engravings. Not much is left from the base sculptures, either. Layers, palimpsests, are the expressions of the paradigms of new civilizations asserting themselves over the old. But here is yet another metaphor of time: the curtain. It deliberately tried to obliterate the earlier traces. The idea was not to open their door but to conceal the door itself. Yet the row of dancing figures survives. Amidst them are my bronze twins, reflected in the mirrors of recovered time in sandstone.

The door unlocks by itself: two dance poses concord in intertwined ecstasy. The movement contained in their arms constellates an open triadic frame. Fusion is umbilical.

> Maidens moving together, with adjacent boundaries,
> Sisters, twins in the expansiveness of the manes
> They kiss—united, of the universe's nodal point
>
> —*Rig Ved*

The one emerging from the undifferentiated zero seeks to replicate itself—as shadow, as light. The egg splits. Form emerges from form. Each splintered part seeks in its multiple trajectories the moment of its indivisibility. The dual heralds its choreography in the play of its mirrors.

The curtain opens. The enigma of my secret self appears.

Overdrive

The path straightens. The road stops to meander, the side tracks seem to cease as the land mass narrows. Site after site, the sculptural patterns lucidly clear, repeating in endless celestial variations—the dance of the twins. Twos and threes, one numerology flowing into another.

What is the vision of the double? What is its meeting point?

A rendezvous of the left and the right?

I am sitting on the left side of the car. In my head, I see the vehicle in front of me suddenly jamming its brakes. I try to warn the driver sitting on my right but I have no voice, and she cannot read the psychic warning in my anguished silence. The car crashes headlong. I awaken. I narrate the dream to the friend who has driven me to Amsterdam from Paris.

Who was the driver? she asks apprehensively.

I excavate my memory for an image, but the image I get is always the same.

She is faceless.

I return to Delhi, and promptly my taxi services are summoned. The brakes are spruced up. It is a beautiful winter morning, the sun is out, the country road is tranquil and the fields appear idyllic as the corn stems waltz to the pleasant breeze. The truck ahead of me beckons me to pass him. Suddenly he changes his mind and jams his brakes.

What is that split second, that moment between nothingness and form, that moment before the great bang, that suspension between life and death? Which way will the balance go—headlong into the cavity below, headlong into the impending crash? Where to now?

127

The dream is razor-sharp—the face stares out at me in the mirror of the moment. I full-brake, but a split second too late. I have veered the car to the left. The crash is not headlong; its impact is diverted.

The mirrors smash, the windscreen smashes, the door caves in on my side. Yet not one flint of glass has scathed us. I step out dazed and enraged. The truck driver is smirking with glee. He casually says he was trying to avoid a stray dog, but there is not a dog in sight.

A young man who has witnessed the entire theatre says angrily to the truck driver: Jaan bujh ke kiya. You did it on purpose.

The truck driver arrogantly shrugs in disdain. Jab maine dekha ke aurat gari chala rahi thi aur baki bhi auratain thi, to panga to lena hi tha. Sabak to sikhana hi tha. Sark mardon ki hai.

When I saw the woman driving and the other women sitting, I had to punish them, teach them their due lesson. The road belongs to men.

I drive on in the battered car. It suddenly strikes me that in Amsterdam, the driver sits on the left.

Rendezvous

The sea breeze beckons from both sides, fuelling the streams of windmills and salt heaps. The hills on the right undulate further into the ground. The land seems to have completely flattened out. There is no other vehicle in sight. A calm descends on me. Twelve years have passed since the dream-accident.

The road belongs to me now.

128

The first drops of water become visible. The coast extends. The tip of the land appears as the seas continue on either side. The waves play in the oceans; their eros elevates me into the bliss of boundary less skies. The navigation of the land I have painfully learnt—I seek the waters now. To dive into their unfathomable depths, ride their waves, float in their cradled curves. Does the journey start anew now?

The sleepy town greets me with its ennui. Day after day the same rising and setting sun, day after day the hordes of tourists arriving for just one vision of the appearing and disappearing sun. How inane and absurd appears the nothingness of their pilgrimages. So what if it provides a livelihood? Life is but the passing of a few split seconds as the sun curves up and down.

The waters have reached their rendezvous as the sun descends into the right, only to rise again from the left. There is no left or right, only the apex of the triangle; even the twins have disappeared into the immaculate amazon, Kanyakumari. Only their umbilical node remains—the waters.

PART III

Hourglass

The heap attains its pinnacle—my journey reaches a climax, its destination. But what is this point of arrival—a moment, measurable like any other? What makes this moment different? A moment not of time passed but of time compressed, a moment that is the sum of all previous instants as the sand heap is a collection of particles?

My driving route has been straightforward, from north to south. It has meandered off the track a little, but still maintained its direction. However, the pilgrimage of time is unchartable—it follows its own course. How does one navigate this invisible maze?

Memory. Where time stands still
Eternally renewing, revealing itself
Infinitizing experience
Dancingly emerging boundlessness
Pure time, pure space
The music of thought
Meandering
Streaming
Harmonizing
Into unknown oceans

Outside a temple site, about midway down the eastern coast, sit a few brahmin beggars. They are psychological masters of faith. Alms are to be coerced. Amidst their rhetoric sits a woman collecting a heap of sand, immersed in her private cosmos, unconcerned with the world outside. When the heap reaches its climax, she slowly spreads it out—even and flat again, as if it recreated the tidal flow of an archetypal hourglass. In fascination I approach her, asking permission to photograph her.

Uttar lo, she answers—take me down, undress me, reveal me—and she beckons to the movement of the sand, quietly alluding to it as the meditative image of existence and nothingness.

Recurrent Leitmotifs

Much like the Moebius strip, where the inner becomes the outer, the outer the inner, the hourglass is a mere cyclic repetition. Direction stands inverted, the up side interchanges with the down side. The process starts anew.

My hankering to reach Kanyakumari matched my childhood passion for mathematics. The point of my destination was simply a recurrent zero, untarnished as the immaculate virgin.

The hourglass inverts. I am no longer southbound; the road curves north. Like a willful river it snakes through small villages, past abundant churches named 'Our Lady . . .' Baby Jesus makes an occasional appearance. The density of traffic, people and animals increases. Lush greenery, coconut groves, the hide-and-seek of the Arabian Sea and the backwaters begins. Water on the left, water on the right as the Gypsy drives over one bridge to the other while the boats plough underneath. Water is a daily companion.

I have driven down with the sea on my left. I drive up again with the sea on my left. Two coasts, one pointed towards the interior, the other more exterior. Adjacent cultures but different languages, histories and even cuisines. The Tamil province is an intricate network of temple site after temple site, apparently built over many centuries. Each period grafted on its own avatars, each period its own intrinsic style. The temples bear no traces of invasion, only the occasional signature of recent distemper—of loudspeakers, of cacophony, of sloth and indifference. Coexistence of times past and times present, coexistence at its best, coexistence at its worst.

The Sanctum

Boundaries have always been known to change. They reflect the fulgurant nature of time, its vagabond spirit. Yet between each line of separation lies the potential of overlapping. Halfway between the two coasts, within Tamil Nadu but belonging to Kerala, is the royal palace of Padmanabhpuram.

A mammoth stone wall surrounded this town, its boundaries resisting access. It blocked Tipu Sultan's invasions into the far south. It sheltered an enclave, a palace—a sanctum.

The sanctum is a protective ring, its residing principle that of immaculate preservation. Its boundaries contain; they are inviolable. They are not to be transgressed.

The palace is an exquisite oeuvre of teakwood, granite, carved rosewood ceilings and a floor made from a marble-like composition of organic extracts, finely powdered shells and coconuts.

I leave the guided tour, the hustle-bustle of populous groups and honeymoon couples. My bare feet glide sensuously over the cool, polished floor. I come into a room, a residential chamber for women. A door leads into a courtyard; a staircase leads to another level. Contiguous spaces on different planes, interconnected. Private chambers to reside in, a chamber where the collections are exhibited, chambers for daily activities, courtyards where the sky enters, exterior and interior simultaneously. Somehow I come to the innermost sanctum, a Devi temple in stone, older than its royal abode—sculpturally similar to Devikapuram.

The temple is still propitiated—in grace, particularly by women. The residing goddess is a form of Sarasvati, the goddess of learning, music and the arts. Ethereal in form, she embodies the razor's edge of consciousness. Riding a swan, she floats on waters wherein is contained the power of meditative remembrance.

Royal power derived itself from this sanctum. It did not replace the sanctum with its earthly opulence and military might; it did not dismantle it or cloak it in whitewashed walls of amnesia. The architecture lay inscribed in a gaze of silent contemplation—the principle of memory in timelessness. Smriti. The sanctum remained its innermost dwelling.

Queen of the Sea

The word *emporium* has a Greek etymology. *Poros* meant passage, voyage; the suffix *ion* designated location. *Emporos* referred to a merchant and traveller.

The word also has antecedents in the old spice route. Passage, the act of carrying over, transferring exotic wares to the marketplace in a major town on crossroads or port, had special significance. Emporiums were the cultural confluence through which different cosmogonies, different journeys of consciousness permeated each other. They were the points that connected the deserts, plains, river valleys, mountains and sea.

Kochi was a major emporium, a natural port on the Malabar coast. Its cluster of islands formed the ocean's open face, connecting it to Arabia, to one countenance of Africa, China and the Far East. The Arabian desert was the vital link between the ports of the Mediterranean and this coast on the Indian Ocean.

Crossing the scorching terrain was an arduous task for which the ancient Arabic-Nabatean civilization was known. It involved an underground knowledge of water sources—entailed camouflaging them, enshrouding them in secrecy for repeated journeys. Astronomy was a way of navigating a geography that had no signposts; the position of the moon and the pattern of the stars and planets paved and guided the way.

A network of cross-cultural hybrid cosmogonies constellated the transformation of an expanse of sand into water—the route from the desert to the sea. Al-lat, the Sumerian goddess, the chthonic Ereshkigal of this underworld, became Al-uzza, the goddess of water sources, and Al-lat, a moon goddess like Venus and the hybrid Aphrodite of Persia and Greece. Mari, the sea goddess, was associated with the dolphins, like her Greek counterpart Dionysus—whose Nabatean twin was the thunder god Duchares.

The openness of the sea contrasts with the backwaters, which descend from the Western ghats. The network of canals creates a labyrinth. There is no easy access; intricate navigation skills are needed. A natural protection that balances the openness of the sea face. Salt water and sweet water side by side, fertile grounds for the monsoons to shower their abundance on the spice plantations.

Pepper, cinnamon, lemongrass were just a few of the natural ingredients that made up the Malabar gold. They appeared to contain a metaphysical presence of life, of its auras, its taste, its aromas. They were its aphrodisiacs. They preserved, they embalmed the dead, they gave taste to frozen meats and their oils burnt in candle lamps, their aromas wafting out.

The Occident lusted after the 'exotic' Orient. Climatic zones were connected—the Nordic cold, the arid heat and the southern monsoons. Cuisine was the quintessential art of life: Its fires fuelled different ways of cooking, of modulating and balancing the freshly ground spices in ever-new patterns of taste. Women were perhaps its guardians.

Coveted wares can lead to a will to power, to control, to complete monopoly. The spice route was no different. The land routes to the north had already been plagued by large-scale invasions, marauding, looting, plunder and genocide. War was ingrained. An absolute god had to be developed, jealous and intolerant, a theology based on military right; the Nabatean goddesses were crushed and sacrificed to its altars. Matrineal traditions disappeared into pasha-like clans. The 'holy war' began, and crushed the very essence of the life it lusted after. Life became a femme fatale whose face it could not bear to see. It transported life into a heaven out of bounds.

The matricide myth is everywhere. Parashuram, Ram with the axe, pledging obedience to his jealous father, beheaded his mother but was filled with the fear of retribution. Each time he bathed in water, the curse came alive: The water mirrored his bloody crime. In disgust he flung his foul weapon, the axe, into the ocean. It broke its own dam, and a flood of water was released. A new land mass, abundantly green, emerged—Kerala.

Kerala is not an easy state to drive in—it is an ongoing density of people. The road goes through one settlement after the other. There is little to differentiate villages, towns and cities. Every now and then, littered at various points on the road, shining-new huge mansions appear, ostentatious exhibits of Gulf money. There are hardly any empty stretches.

Drivers are aggressive, as if they search the murderous thrill of the duel between overcoming and succumbing to time. Signs saying 'Better Late Than Never' and 'Dangerous—Accident Zone' abound, as do overturned speeding buses and trucks at narrow corners.

As the land mass gets wider, the highway between Allappuzha and Kochi starts to open up. A broad, empty stretch . . . I can release the tension in my foot from its proximity to the clutch and brake. The kilometres fly by to the rhythm of the even flow of the accelerator.

The approach road to Kochi is a pleasure of slow driving, of drinking in the curving canals, lagoons and hamlets of a magical old world, only to bring me again to the contemporary urban reality of Ernakulam—part island, part city, more efficient, more liveable, more manageable, less chaotic than other urban centres. And eminently cosmopolitan in flavour, its cafes full of rich cuisine juxtaposed with the ever-growing cyber world. Every now and then, I find architecture with beautiful wooden interiors, where the craftspersonship of the century-old traditions is given sanctity in present time.

I leave my four-wheel-drive in Ernakulam and take the water route of the to-and-fro-plying ferries. The ferries belong to the old world, with their timeless efficiency and punctuality and, of course, their price: a few annas, a few paise to cross to the neighbouring islands. The slow, ambling pace of the boat takes me into a dreamlike reverie.

As I walk through the narrow lanes that circumambulate the canals and lagoons, I have the feeling of consciousness zones blending into each other, much like a well prepared meal whose spices are modulated in accord, balancing each other in a palette of finely tuned harmonies. This is not overcooked meat swimming in a sea of oils and chillis. And the spices are more than a mere metaphor—they are in the air, a permanent ethos. Time stands still and yet moves on, as does the bustling business of the continuing spice trade.

I take the main artery that leads to the central bazaar in Jewtown. There are few Jews left, though the names of the shops bear traces of their past abundance as much as their dwindling presence.

One of the oldest texts goes back to the fourth century, indicating that Jews were given the title of the fifth vannam (caste/class). The philosophy of vannam was a complex conferral and arrangement of spaces that could exist side by side. Architectures of different faiths and 'Weltanschauungen' still exist in apparent compatibility; tourists marvel at this. It is not the law of conversion, of disfiguration of 'idols', of inquisition that reigns but the principle of contiguity.

Contiguous—Touching, Tangential, Bordering Upon

Kochi is its topology. Its geography gave it an open front, while the labyrinthine layout of the backwaters created an impervious interior. The Dutch and Portuguese armadas landed, but they could not penetrate what lay behind the accessible exterior. Even the English could only control the outer part of their island. It was this combination that allowed the Jews fleeing persecution a repeated space of refuge.

The first immigrant landings were over two thousand years ago, but the next waves did not occur till the last millennium. Pogroms in West Asia and the Mediterranean as the result of the Inquisition produced ever newer exoduses.

In 1560, as the Portuguese started establishing their rule in Goa, they set up an Inquisition panel. Jews from within their colonies started coming to Kochi. The raja, who gave them protection, Cheraman Parumal, was referred to by the Portuguese as the 'King of the Jews'.

As I look into the reflection of one of the canals, I seem to see in it its other reflection, another emporium on the sea—Venice, the 'Orient of the Occident'. On this passage, however, Venice is the Occident and Kochi the Orient. The Jews, an artisanal and trading community, were the links on this route as it continued further eastwards. Yet the more I look into this mirror, the more I feel that it is yet another metaphor, another nebulous image that weaves the binding thread. Venice is known for its mist, a mist that seems to enshroud it in a kind of magical time. Here it is the outpourings of monsoon storms that fill up the canals and lagoons. What is it that I see? Another enigma—only a maze of waters.

Gradually I approach the bazaar. What greets me is a surprise: antique shop after antique shop. Many of the iconographies for which I have searched in vain in neighbouring temples are here, curiously displayed in dimly lit interiors. I see a majestic majuscule Lakshmi. Instead of two elephants she has, side by side, two lamps.

A fairy-tale world of lamps seems to open up.

I spot a small figure, an intricately carved woman in bronze, her hands in an open gesture offering a lamp. I fall in love with her. I come into conversation with the shop owner, who belongs to the region. We discuss the histories and complexities of these forms. At some point he asks whether I have financial support for my re-search. I reply in the negative. Eventually I turn to matters of the market and ask her 'price'.

'Rs 2,800.' A momentary lull. 'How much can you afford?' 'Rs 1,200.'

He hands her to me with a soft smile.

'The rest is an offering for your work.'

I saunter further along. The next few shops do not have local owners. They come from the 'north'—from Kashmir. Another kind of contiguity, perhaps, like that of the main attractions here: the Portuguese Mattancherry palace, the 'Hindu' temple adjacent with the synagogue in its backdrop.

As I enter barefoot, it is one image that strikes me above all in the quiet, apparently 'nondescript' synagogue. A multitude of colourful chandeliers and lamps hangs from its ceiling, counterpointing it to the floor of carved blue-and-white tiles, each tile different, brought specially over from China.

I avoid the 'Hindu' temple. Either the gods are asleep and

access is prohibited, or the loudspeakers are jarring. The governing rule is simple: only the gods, or their supposed custodians, may disturb.

The palace is not built on a sanctum. In its architectural confusion, it is loud in its own way. Built by the Portuguese in the sixteenth century as a bribe for the Raja of Kochi in exchange for trading rights, it embodies the imperial seal—and thus could imperial rule and greed set in. Eventually the Dutch replaced the Portuguese, and added their signature to the palace as well. It is an odd medley, a khichdi of exhibits ranging from royal paraphernalia to murals. It is a display where nothing matches, a cuisine with a profusion of rich ingredients but none in synchrony, all in constant collision.

I walk towards the ferry launch. The slow pace, the rhythm of the cradling waters transposes me into a reverie where myth, fantasy and memory seem to blend into each other. I peer out into the horizon, and to my amazement I see their lila—dolphins, playfully leaping up and down in the sea.

Zen and the Sub-marine Fire

Long days of driving. Driving is a kind of Zen meditation, a dhyan, concentration in motion, concentration of motion. One is in its tempo as much as one is a moving observer of tempos going by. Land moves along the water.

Driving is a metier that demands constant attentiveness, meticulous observance of minute details—checking the water, the oil, the air, watching for signs of leakage, listening for sounds of engine variance. It is catching bits of information, studying of maps, working out routes and deciding where to station the Gypsy.

143

I seek a secluded cove, a sheltered angle of the sea. I seek a gaze that comes from a stillness, a gaze that drifts over the horizon of the water, of its unfathomable depth, a gaze that meets the mirror image of my own solitude, which appears as infinite as the stretching sky. A gaze that submerges itself in the adagio-like tempo of slow-changing light as the ball of fire sinks gradually beneath the waters.

Thomas, along with two other friends, runs a different kind of tourism: a small guest house in a small village, bare, with only minimal luxuries—a mosquito repellent called 'Mr Goodnight' and a clean bathroom with running water hot and cold. Thomas cooks Kerala delights, exquisite blends of spices in coconut milk to flavour his juices, lassis and lavish meals. It is an act of love, of finessing a culture. The guest house is not advertised; it is mentioned only to those interested in partaking of and preserving its special fruits. There are no loud cafes, no plastic bottles littering the sea coast, no heaps of overflowing garbage in its coconut groves.

It is a beautiful walk through the grove to the sea, an abundance of streaking birds and the music of their different calls while the sea shimmers in the background. The bay is concordant with my inner image.

The tides recede, the tides extend. They are the pulse of time. No other measures are needed, just the rhythmic sound, sight and feel of the waves.

My gaze is shattered. With murderous lust pouring out of their eyes, saliva oozing out of their mouths, a group of local men indulge in their favourite pastime, a projection that can be thrust on any 'outside free' woman, colour no bar—the rape fantasy.

Later they come to the guest house. Jeering voices, sneering eyes that say it all. A loud altercation. They say the women here are all whores. They demand money.

Milk the foreigners or we terrorize.

Thomas is shattered and ashamed. 'I am not from here; I am from Kochi. Terrible sexual repression. They cannot see women. They cannot respect women.'

Later in the evening, along with the other guest-house residents I go to an old Tantric temple to witness a Theyam enactment. The temple is clean, and open from both sides— one doorway connects it to land, the other to water. The space in-between is a stage on which the avatar descends as the living God in trance. He performs his symbolic dance while the priest offers his aradhana, his salutations. The musicians set the tone while the audience looks on, segregated by gender—men on the right, women on the left. It is a recent phenomenon that women are at all allowed in this all-male stag affair, where the castes are turned on their heads. The avatar enters into the lower-caste man, a tamasic-tamashic guise to which the musicians bear allegiance. The priest, their human servant, belongs to an upper echelon! The prasad is given only to men.

I do not want to belong to this homoerotic transfer, or take on the role of a cold observer or submissive voyeur. It is no compensation for my shattered gaze.

What is the equivalent feminine?

What is its riposte?

A Glowing Fire—Inextinguishable

Once upon a time, the virile mountain propitiates Ganga. She is contemplating her own fire and lightening. She replies

145

that he may only attain her if he can see her primal, timeless, punar form. He agrees, and all four of her river companions, her sakhis, which the rishis stole while she was deep in self-study, are invited. Upon their fusion, Sarasvati, the river surges out. Containing the sub-marine fire, flowing through the current of the mare-fire, she reaches the surface of the earth. The underworld awaits her descent, awaits her shadowy fearful form, which she takes to annihilate the sleazy thieves.

The mountain blocks her flow. He proposes marriage to her. She refuses. He threatens force.

She stipulates that he hold her mare-fire while she bathes. Laughing victoriously, he agrees.

As soon as he touches the fire, he is transformed into ashes. Once more Sarasvati carries the sub-marine fire, and places it into the ocean. The mare-fire, pleased with the safe passage grants her a boon: when the waters are drunk, the mouth is no larger than a needle.

—*Skanda Puran*

An Algebra of Driving Tropes

A desolate, arid, empty stretch that signals bare bleakness. Sparse are the signs of human civilization. It evokes an intense driving memory: I have driven this stretch before, over fifteen years ago. For over a hundred kilometres, the car cruised on a barren road with not even a chai dhaba in sight.

Train journeys, in contrast, are always crowded. Crowded platforms, crowded compartments, crowded stations reflect the mass of human life. In-between the ennui, one seeks to pass the listless time through an inert stare that seeks to lose itself in the landscapes that chugh by.

Train journeys have precise points of departure and arrival. The schedules are fixed, even if they elongate. A long driving journey has a different metaphysics altogether—the gaze is always alert. Each new station becomes a new point, a new turn on a shifting route. There is always an unknown coordinate. The algebra of driving equations is never based on fixed ratios; indefineable are the entities of time and space.

Driving time is the experiencing of different landscapes. Some appear to unfold bit by bit, evolving gradually; some just rush by; others are simply ongoing, with no station in sight. The landscape exists in itself, the human civilizational signature only an empty road.

It is desolate stretches like these that suggest a perpetual austerity. They become the very metaphysics of an interior journey that simply goes on, free of aim—free of expectation—an existential trope of life.

The desolate stretch gives way again to an abundant verdure, estuaries, rivers, as the road runs parallel to the sea. Miniscule islands, the abodes of water birds, abound, accessible only through the slow pace of a boat, much like the elegant, spotless villages connected only by the waterways.

These villages appear relatively unencumbered by the forces of history. The station of Mahe, in contrast, once an imperial stronghold, now lies in lost glory. Belonging to the state of Pondicherry, which lies on the opposite coast, Mahe seems to hang in isolated suspension. Imperial competition gave it a singularity: It was the only French prestige point amidst Dutch and Portuguese domination.

Today, the cracked road says it all—dilapidation. Dilapidated its roads, dilapidated its old houses. The only thing Mahe has to offer is its low alcohol taxes. Wine shops, one after the other. The taste of the local wine says it all: sugar-sweet cough syrup!

Driving has its special moments, its special turning points. Sometimes they are as mundane as finding a carpet-smooth surface after hours of negotiating potholes; sometimes the broadening of a narrow road; sometimes the freedom of a quiet stretch after the density and cacophony of honking traffic. But the moments that inscribe themselves indelibly in the scripts of one's pleasure principles are those in which the driving vista in motion meets the revelation of its surrounding sights/sites. The different coordinates of the changing topologies seem suddenly to achieve a climax, akin to a musical *sam*, when the improvizations of individual instruments suddenly culminate in an ecstatic encounter.

The Gypsy leaves Mangalore, leaves sea level and begins its ascent into the ghats. In elevated motion, the dynamic gaze contains the city, the groves and the sea that expands into the ascent of the ghats. Its overwhelming *jouissance* flows into me.

Connecting Routes, Broken Lines

The road continues over the ghats, up and down like a game of snakes and ladders, coming close to the sea and then climbing up again. It seems to be the connecting thread, like the shoreline that invading forces have broken time and again.

More than any other part of India, this coast was carved up like a Thanksgiving turkey, its parts apportioned like prizes after a ball game. A little piece to the French, a larger one to the Dutch, the larger trophy to the English, but Goa was colonized the longest under the Portuguese stronghold. It makes this small stretch a state apart. There is little trace of its previous histories; the old temples have been dismantled and built over by portentous, pontificating churches that weigh heavily on the small hills. Their heaviness contrasts with the aesthetics of some of the old houses, which are a curious confluence of two sea cultures, the Mediterranean and the Lakshdvip. The doors open out into an introjected gaze on narrow long rooms while the verandahs, the porticoes adorned with a climbing foliage of green frame the projection to the outside, to the sea.

An easy, swimmable sea, a lightness, warm weather, this idyllic ex-hippy coast is up for consumption. Like migratory birds, the chartered flights bring in hordes of sun-tanning tourists escaping ice-cold winters. Natives provide a running service on the beach—cooling juices, coconut water, fruit lassis, cocktails and beer.

The beaches soon acquire distinctive properties. One is filled with deck chairs and a plethora of semi-nude bodies, the other with people who appear grotesquely overdressed. Honeymooning Indian couples muster up their courage and stray into the water. A cabaret of a Bollywood scene—the nightie sticks to the woman's wet skin while the man holds up his pyjama suit. Occasionally groups of men come to ogle the exhibition of skin through binoculars. Twin poles of an equation, perhaps.

But what lies outside this threshold of consumption and discharge of plastic bottles and condoms? How does one receive that other openness of this culture, its sense of ease? Can one make a distinction between the tourist and the traveller?

Travelling is serious work, learning to open out one's senses, to microscopically observe, to perceive the minute details, to hear the varying sounds and sense the changing light. The traveller does not remain, does not leave behind monstrous new constructions. The traveller brings new worlds, brings another gaze, a way of seeing that brings to the surface perceptions long lost in the rootedness of insularity. Above all, it is the moment outside routine, outside comfortable domesticity that allows another meeting point, a contact with the 'extra'—the excess of the ordinary.

The traveller is a sporadic incidence.

Further up, past Goa, driving through the newly planted vineyards on the ghats, I descend on the small, sleepy town of Ganpatipule. The coast seems to stretch out into infinity. The few people appear as insignificant dots overshadowed by an abundance of palm trees. Solitude by the sea in temperate weather is not the arduous solitude of the desert or the elevated sublimation of the high mountains; it is a return to childhood bliss. Hours alone on deserted sea rocks looking for the treasures of their troves, coloured shells and stones, myriads of their patterns, to the rocking, steady sound of the waves. Learning to judge the time through the position of the sun, its light. Above all, forgetting time in the play with water.

The guest house offers no beer, no alcohol, the seafront no cafes. The tourist attraction lies in a little ruined temple on the shore. Every year a mammoth festival is held in honour of its guardian divinity, Ganesh—a mass phenomenon of another proportion. What makes for the magnet of the mass? An event in which it can lose all differentiating boundaries, become one homogenized entity in submission? No individuated self, no silent trance.

Exorcised is the solitude of the stretching sea.

Seven Islands

As I drive through the Deccan plateau, the rugged landscape comes alive: old cave sites atop a hill, alongside a river or simply underground. Much like its Nabatean Other, an incredible network of rock-cut cave architecture—Ellora, Karla, Ajanta, a tapestry of cosmogonies, the Buddhas, the androgyns and the matrikas—wound its way to the sea, a sea that was not then called the Arabian Sea but Lakshdvip (*laksh* = aim/goal, *dvip* = island).

A fisherwoman runs into a winsome tiny temple. Her small, lithe body is in convulsions, in a trance, in rapture, besotted by the presence of a local goddess—Mumba. What lies in her name? What lies in the city that received her name from her—Mumbai? Where is her topology, where is her cosmology in this chawl-stretching, high-rise-elongating, mafia-ridden metropolis?

I have driven into Bombay many times, from the north to the south and the east to the west, but I have little realized its original topology. Now, as I reflect on the change of its name, albeit by an army of human monkeys, it seems to take me into a new journey that results from many older ones.

Islands have a natural protection, their many sheaths of water. Mumbai was not an isolated island but a sacred archipelago graced by the number seven—a collection of seven islands. It was governed by the trinity of goddesses: Mahakali, Mahasarawati, Mahalakshmi. What a jewel, what a diamond,

151

what a Kohinoor was this gift, this dowry given by the Portuguese in the name of the imperial alliance between Catherine de Braganza and Charles II! This was not to be a small island like the one the vainquers had come from. A new challenge, a new potential, a new fantasy was to be unleashed in full might. And what lay at their disposal but an old civilizational intelligence, artisanal expertises in exile, waiting to unfold?

Not linguistically talented, the English had little taste for the pronunciation of local names. They altered them according to a curious random principle: any way they liked. The good bay, as it had been christened by the Portuguese—Bom Bahia— became the beginning of a grand project. The islands would no longer remain suspended in water but would be connected to each other, land into water, to build the industrial dream. They would become the Gateway to India, the new Victorian city, the imperial capital of commerce. Banias, Jews, Parsis, Bohras, Khojas were induced to move. Artisans, the mistrys, traders, the shipbuilding community shifted from Diu, from Surat to these harbours. Cosmological architecture gave way to a new engineering feat: Water was transformed into land. A new causeway was constructed. The seven islands became one land mass.

An idyll gone awry! I search for hours for the solitary rock front on which I played for hours as a child, but the sea is only an ethereal memory. Banished, vanished like a Gogia Pasha sleight of the hand, Gilly Gilly come, Gilly Gilly go. What could he not make appear and disappear, coins jingling, birds in hand, birds in flight? An array of young beautiful women would appear onstage, suddenly become invisible, then emerge from the rear . . . that was his particular speciality. Once a child got so upset at this desertion that she started sobbing, and the hypnotic trance was broken, the gown of invisibility shed. One woman was seen calmly walking to the other side. An accident, a trick that went too deep into the emotions, so deep that it revealed its power and its antidote.

The islands-city was to produce a new gold, a new colonial currency: cotton. The age of the spice and silk routes was over! Handloom, the century-old weaving arts were to be replaced by industrial mills. What an act of magic! Trade was no longer a question of exchange; the new 'equation' was building surplus. Produce raw material with the expertise in the colonies, then ship it out and bring it back at over double its original price.

The mills attracted workers from the south, from the land. From an initial population of a few thousand, the surplus created a multi-fold increase that continues to continue. Yet a part of the new island remained an enclave—the lords had their seaside promenade, their exclusive clubs, their marine drive while the natives had the 'black' city.

The sea disappears into a stinking open lavatory. The full, mass potential of the British dream, perhaps! Chawl after chawl, high-rise after high-rise; the united land mass is a magnet. Ongoing migration: The more land is reclaimed, the more human density threatens to explode any lines of demarcation. Marine Drive is an expression of this democratic chaos—its promenade, its divergent moods, its peddlers, its beggars, its street urchins, people of all hues and shapes. I stare out into a fading horizon. The water is murky.

An old competitiveness reigns between the two capital cities, one political, one commercial. 'Bombay' is India's largest factory of fantasies gone askew, the drama of the world transposed to a stage of artificial sets. Repeated melodramas construed on to a formula ad absurdum, overused emotions becoming a vaccine against any passionate feeling, any raw touching of life.

For a long time, I thought the main difference between Delhi and Mumbai lay in the fact that Mumbai was a new city, devoid of an earlier history. Delhi went back thousands of years, the fulcrum of one river-valley civilization after another. Which new ruler had not made Delhi its capital? Ruins everywhere, ruins scattered from different time zones, century upon century, a labyrinth of old stones that seemed ironically to counterpoint the neat criss-crossed lines laid out by Her Majesty's enterprise. A royal path, a broad avenue that led to Parliament and a people's path that has now sprawled out into the beyond, over the pale of its seven cities, over the river.

Seven seems to be the number that links the two metropolises, as does the origin of their names. *Delhi* also comes from the name of its protective deity, the devi Dhillika. The Greek word *metropolis* seems fitting: *meter* = mother, *polis* = city. But the lens of time has blurred this link, has superimposed images of another fiction in which one can only imagine the topos of the older narrative through an inner eye.

The eye starts to chisel away, layer after layer. What does it start to see? The play of light and water reflections on an old tree; a man sitting for hours by a little lake feeding fish. Every now and then, a goose comes up to him and arrogantly receives its tiffin. A mesmerizing activity, throwing little pieces of atta in the clear water and watching the fish dart away at it. A habitual timepass meditation.

Mumbai's little lake, Banganga, is a sheltered spot to which one descends a flight of steps from a crowded road. A natural spring, it is said to be an underground link to a network of rivers. Incredible banyan trees, roots hanging to the ground, winding threads bind the sky to the subterranean. I climb a little hill on the other side and find that it overlooks a tiny cove. The small piece of land is a rubbish heap. I start to erase it. I descend and walk up another set of stairs. A broken-down house, but the carving is there—a snake figurine. Old temple remnants. Minute leftover traces.

I am writing a new kind of parchment. Not a palimpsest, not an overwriting, but rather a rubbing-out till the obscure detail emerges.

The crowded, maddening traffic intersection gives way to a towering silence as the taxi turns half left. Meher takes me into the Zoroastrian temple, a place of stillness. A curious silence accompanies the grove of trees and the carefully nurtured garden. Flowers of different colours bloom.

Access to the grove is out of bounds; only the near ones of the deceased may go in at the stipulated time. A preserve for vultures, with constant carrion to nurture them. People in the card-like buildings disappearing in the haze of the sky complain—Eccentric old habits. A time zone out of synchrony, the secluded area seems to have that obscure trace, the hanging tree roots, the hanging garden. It makes the idea of Persepolis come alive.

Persepolis destroyed, its civilization in ashes . . . the birds in flight looking for Simorgh, the 'idol'-worshippers, the 'fire'-worshippers in flight from the mindless violence of a conquering prophet. Born of a woman, Dughdova, fecundated by a shaft of light, a milky way of light, Zarathushtra was assigned the role of protecting this source, this light—this fire. Sixteen different kinds of fire, and many more undisclosed forms. A complex of angels of many genders, a cosmology of fire finely individuated and differentiated. An ancient theology of years of solitude in the recesses of the desert.

After the sacred fire's arduous journey across the sands, over the sea, through countless dangers, through a thousand years of time, it landed in Diu. Here, in this grove of banyan trees, the light shimmering through their roots, it seems to alight on the disappearing ink of faded memory.

A decreasing population, while that of the city has multiplied more than thousand-fold in four hundred years, from ten thousand to more than ten million. I look at the glasswork on the windows of old Parsi houses. I look at their thatched verandahs, different from those on mammoth Victorian Gothic architecture, at their opera house crumbling in lost glory.

An equally mammoth undertaking was the railway line that was to connect the waterway to the land way, Victoria Station to the Gateway of India. Simply VT now, ferrying passengers and tiffins while ferries ply away from the Gateway— a vaudeville tamasha of peddlers' theatre. An incredible art, from the will to the survival of life. What a sleight of hand!

One peddler is selling puppets that appear to miraculously move on their own, performing whimsical dances—capriccios.

Like his burqa-clad wife, the pasha is enthralled, incredulous. They really move by themselves!

Yes. and they can do what you wish.

Good business, I smile at him. Perhaps I should ask him for his story, the mystery of the strings so fine that one does not see the hands that move them. One only sees the doll-like gesticulations.

The survival-of-life texture is a richness few countries can boast. Refugee narratives of pogroms and poverty: Someone came in a crowded train, someone walked many roads . . . a sea of refugees in the sea of time from Persia, from Iraq, from Sind, from Armenia, from Europe, from the neighbouring states, people everywhere, in every nook and corner. A young beggar boy takes time off to hang his bricoleur swing of a rotten cycle tyre from the branch of the tree. Away, away in the wind he swings, away.

'Away, away in the wind,' sings a shrieking, out-of-tune soprano voice. Its owner: a dark skinned Anglo-Indian named Miss Rondo, in a classroom of my abandoned Convent of Jesus and Mary. She teaches the art of Her Majesty's correct elocution.

What is the way in this wind? What is the way in this fog of maze? What is the way in this thicket of human mass?

Chuckling, a Russian-Israeli woman caps her response to my India stories by elocuting the words of a sign on a local temple:

People not allowed. Only broken coconuts.

Kaleidoscope of the Seven

> She, winding serpentlike, the splendid thunderous Sarasvati,
>   the seven, the mother of Sindhu
>
> She, of the fragrant fluids, flowing serenely, full with her own
>   waters
>
> —*Rig Ved*

Seven is an enigmatic number. Like the Moebius strip, it makes visible the invisible, invisible the visible—source of a strange maya—an incredible repertoire of magic, a transforming lila, a kaleidoscope.

Kaleidoscope, from the Greek: *kal* = beautiful, *eido* = shape. The kaleidoscope is an optical instrument consisting of a rotating tube, mirrors and loosely held bits of colourful glass. With each movement, the shapes and patterns of glass change.

The seven transforms water into land and land into water. Islands disappear, returning to the abysmal depths of the ocean while the earth trembles to release them, along with their waters, again.

Where does the seven take me? Where to does this winding thread take me next? What mire of water and land must one cross to attain a new threshold? What razor's edge of consciousness awaits, what maryada?

I drive along the sea coast, along the Gulf of Khambhat to the peninsula of Kathiawar. My research indicates a number of ruined Chamunda temples off the coast. The maps are old, and like their changing names, they no longer tally with the movement of time. Learning to read old maps, to find their approximate location on a modern road map and then actually find the sites is a kind of science, a learning of new local names, their variations and phonetics, and of a correlating them to times past.

I locate a small village called Miani and find an old ruined temple, magnificent in its framing of light. Eight pillars constellate an open verandah, roofless, the spaces between them transparent with light. They lead to a small yoni shrine in which an opening to the ground is visible. The shrine lies in semi-darkness. One pours water into an opening that flows underground. One emerges back into a circular arc of light framed by the pillars.

Intoxicated by the experience, I push my luck and try to find yet another site. I locate the village and the villagers lead me to an old baba, ancient in appearance, and a ruined temple renovated in the usual modern garb(age) of plaster and bathroom tiles. The baba is awaiting his unknown visitor. He invites me to afternoon tea. The tea comes in a little cup atop an equally miniscule saucer. He pours half the tea in the saucer and offers it to me. I talk to him in Hindi and he replies in Hindi, not in Gujarati as is often the case.

Was there an old Chamunda temple here?

Who is Chamunda? Yahan pe to khali khandhar tha. Basti bhi nahi thi, log bhi nahi the.

Here there was only a dilapidated ruin. There was not even a little settlement, not even any people.

Fota-album dekhoge?

I nod expectantly.

The fota album turns up—fota after fota of a shining piece of metal dressed in red. A middle-aged woman offers flowers while the baba performs other rituals. A nice family album.

He starts to narrate his story in laconic details. I glean an

159

incomplete gist. For some traumatic reason, he decided to drop out from the 'world' and walk out of his birth state, Haryana. He walked and he walked, he walked many days, many months till he came to this khandhar, to this ruin. Meanwhile, the woman in the fota album was also wandering; their paths met and the khandhar became their abode. Gradually, as local people started migrating, they received their daily due of some tea and a little food every now and then. Slowly, with small contributions, the khandhar was made pucca, like the pucca sahibs—solid and cooked.

But then his companion left in a state of samadhi. She shed her human body.

Ab to ek hi intazar hai. Bas us hi ka intazar hai, jo meri jagah lesakhega, he says to me in winsome expectancy.

I await just one thing now—the person who can take my place.

We both know, in that moment, that we have not quite found what we are looking for.

As an afterthought, to make up for his disappointment, he asks, with yearning in his voice—nostalgia written on his face—'Do you speak English?'

Yes.

Can we speak some English? I get homesick for the language. There is no one to talk to here . . . so I put on the radio and listen to cricket commentary.

Dropouts are essentially wanderers. Wandering is a strange metier, a sense of being a flaneur in the world. One walks about, one roams around, one has curious accidents, one has curious collisions, one has curious coincidences, one has curious encounters.

P approached me in a small mountain hamlet, Manikaran. Parvati's earring, her kundalini, is said to have fallen here. Ethereal fire in water, mists of steam rising out of the cascading waters, out of the valley—the mountains stand cloaked in them, draped in them. The sulphur burns, the steam cooks the raw food, cleanses the body while the fast-flowing surging river cools the frenzy.

P had made his way from Brazil. His Jewish ancestry was from different continents. He gave up his profession, engineering, to wander in the world. He worked as a taxi driver in New York to raise some capital; then he made his way to Southeast Asia and across the sea to the Indian coast. He cycled from the south up to the northern plains and is now trying to find his way to another mountain village, Malana.

Malana is a secluded mountain village with its own language and its own code. Everyone who comes from the outside into its vicinity is an untouchable. For every accidental touch, an animal must be sacrificed, for which the outsider must pay. Money must not be touched, either; it can only be flung across.

The climb is as steep as the gorge is narrow. There is no cement road, no wide path, only a tenuous serpentine ascent over cascading waterfalls. The mountainsides are cloaked in virgin forests and the sound of the rushing torrential river reverberates in their bosom, in the rustling of their leaves. Wild cannabis grows in free abandon.

Exhausted, we arrive as the light starts to dim into a metallic blue. There is only one room where we are permitted to stay: at the home of the local untouchable, a Negi. He is originally from Kinnaur, the Far East of the Indian Himalayas, bordering Tibet. His long ancestral journey was made on foot many

161

decades ago. The room is tiny, dark, dingy and filled with travellers—an Australian, a German, a local French, a local Italian and the four of us. Just enough room for each to stretch out a sleeping bag.

The chelum is passed around, its warmth wafting through the weaving stories of a Decameron. The local Italian is a jovial, kind middle-aged man who speaks Hindi. Many years ago, he threw his Italian passport away into some heap of snow and made his home in a nearby cave, where he embroiders little purses. Every now and then he is able to sell them to visiting tourists, but his needs are basic; food is no issue, and the chelum is always full.

And have you no nostalgia?

None whatsoever.

The conversation changes to food, to finding a good cafe after days of dal-roti, to buona pasta and good cheese. The Cupid-like arrow of ardent longing, nostalgia, has made its way to the stomach of our Italian friend.

What is the propelling emotion that makes one travel, that makes one explore, what is that pre-condition of exile and what is the desire of nostalgia, the compelling pain of longing of return to what source, to what lost idyllic zero?

The road continues westward, parallel to the coast. The area has been afflicted by drought, yet the sight of water is so resplendent. But water itself seems to reflect that quality of time—its transience, its moments of transit, stations of life.

Seven is the state of being transitory, being between thresholds and crossing from one to another.

This area, tucked away in the arc of the Gulf of Khambhat, is filled with sites. The many-millennium-old harbour of Lothal lies here, a civilization famed for its knowledge of water, its intricate canalization within the topos of its polis and outside it towards the sea. Water circulated here, within and without, creating neither surplus nor stagnant discharge. Today there is no sea, no water in the many canals. There are mere reminders. The coastal lines, too, are in transience.

I follow the line of my time. It takes me to a small village off the famous point of Somnathpur. I find a small temple that has survived the Ghazni invasion. The local villagers are suspicious of it.

Randiyon ka mandir hai.

The temple belongs to the prostitutes.

The sculpture is intact, the signature of the triadic feminine explicit. I locate a small underground cave. The opening is so narrow that I can barely squeeze in. I descend into the womb-like space. A local man has appropriated it and, as the self-styled priest, demands his tax—Rs 10. He is proud of his creation, his usurped temple. His life oeuvre has been to have gaudy, parrot-green bathroom tiles put on the cave's walls.

I ascend to another cave, part of a contiguous array of small caves above and below. In the clearing adjacent stands the temple. The cave leads to yet another gateway, a torana—an old stepwell. As I descend the steps, a little niche stares out at me. In it sits a sculpted figure, a Devi in lotus position, padma-asan, oblivious to all and sundry.

Stepwells seem to be my guide. They seem to quench my thirst for memoric water, to reveal the different narratives of unfinished memories.

I arrive in Dwarka, another place where baby Krishn is said to have been born. A mammoth, fairly recent temple stands in the main square; next to it is the small, millennium-old base of a Devi temple and an adjoining stepwell. The well has just been excavated, and its sweet water has been the saving grace for local drought-induced thirst.

Underground goes the journey into the concealed abysses, into the padlocked crypts, into the vaulted subterranean chambers. Deep-sea diving, marine archaeology, acoustic underwater images reveal Lothal-style ruins akin to temples, granaries, an acropolis and a great bath.

The stepwells are great baths. Pools of water, a collection of water that falls from the sky, a mosaic of finely woven rivulets sprung from an underground source. A place for wayfarers to replenish themselves, a place for reflection, a place for immersion, a place for renewal of one's own fluids, a place for liminal play, a confluence of the sacred and the worldly.

Underground temples are littered all over, forming a unique route that continues north from present-day Gujarat and Rajasthan. They are the only kind of architecture still credited to queens. Despite the invasions of their sculptures and figurative forms, many survived thanks to the reigning queens.

The stepwell in the vicinity of Ahmedabad lies adjacent to a mosque constructed later. The queen revived the waters, restored the sanctity of their architectural home, but the dynamic scale of the graphics, the figurative sides was obliterated. They became abstract ornaments, repeated repeatedly in a placid homogeneity.

Variations in graphic forms, their depictions in expressive faces, in sinuous lines of the body are akin to a musical scale.

The notes are modulated to fine precision, dropping to a very low base and ascending again to the tip, a high pitch—an apex. Each note, each minute variance is in relation to another, each interval a musical moment. Carefully wrought graphic symbols in individuation are in rapport to the different perspectives of life, to the strange mystery of faces, to the expressions embodied in them. The source, their centre, is the flow of water.

I follow the stepwells' route in time, in space. They take me to the old river Sarasvati, to the old cities that extend in a circuitous line from Lothal to Dholavira, Harappa and Mohenjo-daro. At least four thousand years old, the sites are like points on the coast, points on the river. Today one side is partitioned from the other; Kutch is split from Sind. A rupture, a fracture that seems to tear the land apart, to break the flow of the river, the coast.

Their route takes me to the queen of all stepwells, the temple in Patan. Excavated only recently, it still seems so intact—the form preserved, the faces on the sculptures revealed, detail after detail, a choreography of life in stone. Steps lead from one layer, one level to another. One echelon does not erase the previous one; it is merely an initiation. Their number is not arbitrary. It is seven.

The seven fused, one wagon, one wheel,
One mare propelling the seven names;
The three navels of the undecaying wheel,
Never to be constrained;
The existence of the world.

This wagon, thus the existence of the seven,
The wheel of seven, pulled by seven mares;

The seven sisters, collectively evoking the cows,
Celebrating themselves when the seven names are proclaimed.

—Rig Ved

Of the seven, thus the luminous shadow, the reflection in the
   mirror,
Through the reflection, the splendour of the three-path, she
   the ever-renewable

—Devi Upanishad

The name of Sati evolved from a mathematical abstraction.
Her root is *sat*—seven. The dramaturgy of her mythology takes
on the corresponding properties of twists, turns and trans-
formations. Sati is overcome by a nostalgia for her primordial
form, for a return to the matrika of the 'pleasure principle.'

Sati breaks the law of the 'father'—she turns into a shadow
form, a living corpse, an intensity of sexual heat, an aspect of
Kali, Ugrachanda, that refuses to burn in Daksh's sacrificial
fire, in its exorcised 'purification.'

Ugra-chanda or she (of the) form of eighteen hands,
She of the foremost nine fusing in the light/heat of the dark
lotus of kanyas

—Kalika Puran

The heat lets loose its flames. An alchemy of elements takes
place—a deluge of water surges out.

A rain [vrishti] of flowers takes place and the sacrificial site
is transformed into a cremation ground [shamshan ghat]
with the wolves and jackals of Kali having a feast day eating
the remnants of those present.

—Mahabhagvat Puran

The made-manifest (pradur-bhuta) mahamaya with her band of yoginis, during the autumnal full moon creates twelve yearly cycles of rain to deluge all those present/invited at the sacrifice at Daksh's gathering.

—*Kalika Puran*

The demure consort has disappeared into thin air; only a vacant carcass remains. Shankar is desolate. In mourning, he carries the empty body. He dances in limitless frenzy, in an abandon of pain. Meanwhile the yoginis dance in wild ecstasy.

The gods are fearful. Vishnu starts to sever the body of seven. Her laughter falls, her earrings fall, her mind falls, her cheeks fall, her eyes fall, her hair, her cheeks, her yoni falls. They fall on to the deserts, on to the plains, into the valleys, into the mountains and on to the hilltops. Wherever the parts fall, cosmic sites emerge—Sati's seats, her piths, her citadels, her acropolis.

acro = tip, height, topmost
polis = city

Stairs that go below also go above. Each stepwell seems to have its hilltop. Up and down I climb, two thousand steps, three thousand steps—Pavagadh, Palitana and Junagadh, to cite just a few sites. Some part of the seven seems to have plummeted here.

Then the steam being in the middle of the ocean fuses

The receptacle containing water, of past existence,

The boundaries/shores, touching points are the two forms of yours (Sati)

167

Diverging/altering shores, steam in the middle of the island of lotuses

The river becoming the vaitarani (river linking earth with underground), going into and becoming the first ocean.

—*Mahabhagvat Puran*

Point of Return

The Gypsy speeds on the newly enlarged highway. The voyage of the seven, the route of stepwells brings me back safely to Delhi.

The old city of Lal-kot is strewn with stepwells, but one of my favourites lies outside its peripheries. It is in the centre of Delhi, concealed by high-rise buildings. They have eaten into its water level. Its gates are often shut; the chowkidar has an alcohol problem and simply does not show up to open it to the few-odd visitors who occasionally come. Sometimes I am lucky and can rent a ladder from some of the local people. One of the men informs me that two-odd decades ago he used to dive and swim in it. It too has the signature of seven, but no sculptures survived the genocide.

Genocide and mass exodus seem to have marked the city of my birth, a modern city dominated by a culture of refugees. Yet each civilization has left its traces behind. Perhaps that is the paradox of the city, so ancient and yet possessed of a hankering rootlessness of which I seem to be no exception.

A peripatetic itinerant, I started a strange journey in which I knew a certain destination of my pilgrimage, the tip of the land and the confluence of the ocean waters. But where is the point of return, what is the optimal home to which I return?

Delhi, the natal station; Indonesia, where my foetus formed; Sind and Multan, from whence my ancestors came—*Where?* is always the question that the journey poses. Where is the beyond of the cycle that comes to culmination? Where is the climax after the climax?

A solitary kingfisher has made its way to my terrace in Delhi and made its perch there. It is rare to see a kingfisher in a place that has no water. There are no fish. It seems to speak to me in another language, it seems to offer me another book—*A Symphony of Birds.*

Finale—Allegro Giusto

The brilliant moonbeam, turquoise-cloaked
Soaring atop the wide oceans
Over the mountain peaks

The kingfisher emits an enchanting call
the nightingale sings in crescendo

Where are my wings?
Where is my magic wand?

That I may follow their spiralling path
Listening to their haunting melodies

Fly my friend, into the clear azure skies
Fly my friend, on to the carpet of dazzling stars

Land my friend, in the silken valley of rainbow-coloured
flowers

Wild Cannabis Emanates from Flight

The phoenix was a mythical bird of great beauty. It lived in the savage Arabian deserts. Each time it was burnt on a funeral pyre, it re-emerged more resplendent than ever.

The moment Sati leaves her body on the funeral pyre, she undergoes yet another transformation.

svayam-antarhita bhutva gaganam asthita

In becoming of the state of svayam-antarhitathe, the concealed self, the goddess is of the state of the skies/heavens.

—Maha Bhagvat Puran

I leave my driving journey for yet another journey into the climax of this myth. The seven of water leads me to the source of Sati, Parvati—her archetypal form, Parvati = parvat = mountains.

The mountain stream, the river flows in yet another valley, the valley of Sangla in the land of Kinnaur. A dominantly matri-lineal people emerging from one origin, one family name—Negi. Kinnauris were mythical creatures, part human, part animal and part bird. They were capable of flight. It was part of another route, the silk route that linked the higher plateau of Spiti and Tibet to China and Mongolia.

Sind and Multan are embodied in a layer of West and Central Asian histories, particularly ancient Persian mythologies. My grandmother from one side had a passion for languages—Persian and Arabic belonged to her repertoire. But my childhood was filled with fairy tales from the Nordic world, snow queens, elves, goblins and, above all, fairies. Is there a route, a silken carpet that connects these magical archetypes? Is there a point of return there/here?

The Magical Feather

Late one moonless night, the magical feather of Simorgh is said to have dropped in China.

Simorgh in her early forms was a curious bird-creature. A kind of monstrous peacock, a sphinx, a winged lion, protectrix of seeds, flowers and plants, nursemaid of the Persian prince Zal. She looked after the abandoned baby and gave it yet another name: Dastaan, Destiny, the Trickster of life and death.

Simorgh later became the sovereign king, his sight the aim of the hazardous journey undertaken by the birds through seven valleys.

The river that flows through the Sangla valley flows into China while the land above it becomes a rooftop desert—arid, austere, with hardly a tree in sight. Sparse are the villages that mark this awesome terrain. The high mountains tower, the snow gleams in the clear blue of the skies. Human life is a mere dot, insignificant in its transient finitude. The monasteries are a testimony to the overwhelming solitude of existence. Time seems to stand frozen in the snow-bound villages. No access to the outside, no access from the outside; brief are the months when the barren jeep track is driveable. It takes me to a small village at the end of the road to the Indo-Tibetan border. An army soldier sits pensively on the mountainside. He seems impregnated with the long days of waiting for time to pass. He strikes up a conversation with me.

Philosophically he says, doing his duty: You can photograph this mountain but not that. It's for border security. This mountain belongs to India, that mountain to China.

Lifting the Veil—The Face of Simorgh

A mountain pass is a narrow route across a relatively low notch or depression in a mountain barrier. It is a door that opens one range to another—no divisions, no national boundaries, only clouds afloat a carpet of light, a sky that seems to stretch out into the horizon of infinity. Snowflakes fall as I start to walk slowly to the small clearing that marks the Kunzam pass, 4,600 metres high. Yet it seems to be a kind of bridge between the land far below and the mountains that soar above. They appear so close and yet are beyond touch. Snow lies in their bosom. They are the Himalya, the abode of snow, of its light: *him* = snow, *alya* = abode.

Small pieces of cloth hang on a small temple, quivering in the whistling wind. A large black stone lies outside. It is said that if one puts a coin on it and the coin sticks, one's wishes will be fulfilled.

Above the stone is a small cupboard. The glass door is closed with a latch. A figure lies within, draped in white cloth.

I open the latch, push open the door and slowly remove the veil of white. The goddess Kunzam sits there, bedecked with a crown of skulls atop a horse-mule and, further below, an inverted male figure.

> The first-said, the daughter of the ether-mountain, the first pairs of eight yoginis, their cycle and respective fusion are the sixty-four yoginis.
>
> —*Kalika Puran*

Is it the face of Simorgh that I see there/here?

There in the Simorgh's radiant face they saw
Themselves, the Simorgh of the world—with awe
They gazed and dared at last to comprehend
They were the Simorgh and the journey's end.

—Farid-ud-Din Attar,
The Conference of the Birds

Shunya Ghar Basti—The Mirror Abode

But there appears to be a cupboard within the cupboard. It introjects into an even smaller interior chamber. The glass doors are without frames. They swivel in and out. An ethereal light refracts through the translucence; it seems to contain fine particles of timelessness. Only the face in its mirror is invisible, without form, without features. It seems to be an abstraction of all forms, an abstraction beyond abstraction, a maya beyond measure.

It is the face of zero, of shunya.
It has a unique enigma.
It is indivisible.

Other books from Spinifex Press

Goja

Suniti Namjoshi

This powerful meditation, part autobiography, part elegy, deconstructs the glamour given to wealth and power and celebrates the quest for love.

ISBN 1-875559-97-3

Building Babel

Suniti Namjoshi

A fabulous new book in which time, space and the discipline of love come under scrutiny.

Suniti Namjoshi is an inspired fabulist: she asks the difficult questions—about good and evil, about nature and war—unfailingly bracing her readers with her mordant humour and the lively play of her imagination. —Marina Warner

ISBN 1-875559-56-6

Feminist Fables

Suniti Namjoshi

An ingenious reworking of fairytales. Mythology mixed with the author's original material and vivid imagination. An indispensable feminist classic.

Her imagination soars to breathtaking heights.
—Kerry Lyon, *Australian Book Review*

ISBN 1-875559-19-1

St Suniti and the Dragon

Suniti Namjoshi

Ironic, fantastic, elegant and elegiac, fearful and funny. A thoroughly modern fable

It's hilarious, witty, elegantly written, hugely inventive, fantastic, energetic.
—U. A. Fanthorpe

ISBN 1-875559-18-3

If you would like to know more about Spinifex Press,
write for a free catalogue or visit our website

Spinifex Press
PO Box 212 North Melbourne
Victoria 3051 Australia
<http://www.spinifexpress.com.au>